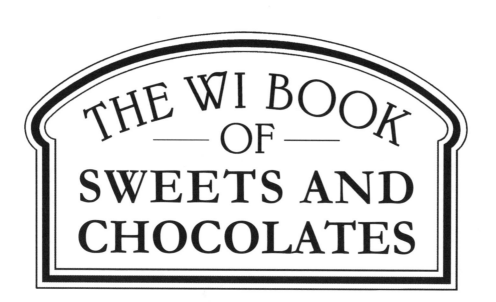

THE WI BOOK OF — OF — SWEETS AND CHOCOLATES

compiled by
**Margaret Clift   Irene Green
and Dilwen Phillips**

WI BOOKS

Copyright © National Federation of Women's Institutes
First Published 1999 by WI Books

in association with Stable Ltd
Glebe House, Church Street,
Crediton, Devon EX17 2AF

Illustrated by Michael Lye

British Library Cataloguing in Publication Data.
A CIP catalogue record for this book is available from the British Library.

ISBN 0 947990 57 7

Printed and bound in Great Britain by Short Run Press Ltd, Exeter, Devon

CONTENTS

CONTENTS

CONTENTS

INTRODUCTION

Sweets are a treat, and home-made confections can be a special delight, evoking nostalgic reminders of the old-fashioned favourites that seem almost to have disappeared in the present age of mass production. They are food for sheer pleasure – in the making, tasting and giving. With a little personal artistry in the presentation, they can easily be lifted into the luxury class, rewarding you with the admiration and pleasure of the recipient.

With so much awareness today of the need for healthy eating, sweets and choco- lates have gained the reputation of junk food, yet sales of them do not seem to diminish. It is hoped with this book to persuade you that by having control over the choice of good quality ingredients, when producing your own home-made confections, whether they are old favourites or new and unusual delights, that the results can be both satisfying and wholesome.

WHAT IS INCLUDED AND WHY

The book has been written with both the novice and experienced sweet-maker in mind. It is important to understand the properties of sugar and the changes that take place as the cooking temperature increases. Before using the recipes, spare a little time to read the introduction and understand the processes involved.

There are basic recipes for each type of sweet. Variations have been included and, with experience, you will introduce your own modifications. Many of the recipes can be adapted for use with the microwave – this comes with experience.

A little imagination with the presentation of the finished sweets can turn the ordinary into the extraordinary. Instructions for making containers have been included, but sweets can also be presented in a poke, a rolled container made of greaseproof or cellophane, similar to an icing bag, or on a plain plate, on Crown Derby or Spode, in a mug, glass or container with a lid – experiment yourself.

EQUIPMENT

Equipment for sweet-making is basic and simple; probably the keen cook will have the necessary utensils already in her kitchen. However, there are a few items that will contribute notably to success. The first four are essential; the last two are strongly recommended.

Saucepans
A selection of various sizes. These should be of good quality and deep. A shallow pan is more likely to cause the contents to burn. A deep pan enables more correct readings when a sugar thermometer is used. Copper, stainless steel and aluminium are all suitable and should have firm, thick bases to withstand the heat required of certain mixtures and to ensure its even distribution.

Spoons
A selection of both wooden and metal spoons, which should be kept exclusively for sweet-making. Wooden spoons are easier to handle when beating mixtures and also do not conduct heat in the same way as metal spoons when used to stir very hot syrups.

Spatulas
Useful for working fondants and turning cooling syrups, barley sugar, etc.

Pastry Brush
This is for washing down sugar crystals from the sides of the pan while sugar is dissolving. It should be a good quality wooden brush and kept solely for confectionery purposes.

Marble Slab
This is ideal, if available, for working hot syrups, as some kitchen work surfaces do not withstand the heat of certain mixtures. The top of an old-fashioned washstand is perfect, if you are lucky enough to be able to find one.

Sugar thermometer
Though it is not absolutely essential to use one, a thermometer is advisable, particularly when exact temperature readings are needed. They are not expensive and soon prove their worth by eliminating guesswork; they can also be used for preservation.

Moulds
Rubber moulds for fondant sweets; plastic moulds for chocolates.

Dipping fork
For dipping chocolates.

Skewers
For dipping chocolates.

Kitchen scissors

Tins
A variety of square or rectangular tins. Baking tins are suitable.

Cutters
Petits fours cutters.

Dropper
For measuring flavourings accurately.

Stationery
(a) Foil
(b) Greaseproof, silicone or waxed paper
(c) Petits fours cases

INGREDIENTS

Ingredients should be of the best quality available if the results are to be nutritious and delectable.

Fats
(a) *Butter* may be salted or unsalted. Salted butter is stronger flavoured and the salt is virtually undetectable in the finished result. Lightly salted butter is usually preferred. Concentrated butter, obtainable in larger supermarkets, can be used very successfully, especially in fudges, as it contains less water and therefore boiling time can be reduced. Butter gives a creamy flavour.

(b) *Margarine* may be substituted in very small quantities but it is less easily absorbed than butter.

Sugar
All types may be used but most sweets use granulated or caster sugar. Brown sugar and demerara sugar have distinct flavours.

Honey
Some recipes benefit from its special flavour but it is expensive to use in quantity.

Golden Syrup and Treacle
Used for their distinct tastes.

Glucose

This is needed to prevent sugar syrups from crystallizing. Powdered glucose is ideal in fondant creams and fudges and is available from chemists and drug stores. Liquid glucose can be bought from cake-decorating and sugarcraft outlets.

Milk, condensed and evaporated

These contain less water than fresh milk and therefore less boiling time is needed to evaporate the liquid.

Eggs

(a) Whole eggs: fresh eggs may be used if the mixture is cooked; eg. in some truffle recipes.
(b) Egg white: only use if the mixture is cooked, otherwise replace with …
(c) Egg albumen – follow the manufacturer's instructions.

Flavourings and Colourings

Use natural flavours and colours wherever possible – the zest of oranges and lemons for citrus flavours. Fruit purées, concentrates or, occasionally, fresh fruit preserves are acceptable. Bottled flavours from the grocers are useful. 'Oils' are preferable to 'Essences', where available, as the flavour is natural and more concentrated. Flavourings should not be added before the cooking is completed, as they will evaporate in the boiling. If you can smell it, it is evaporating and weakening. Colours should always complement the flavour.

Combined colouring and flavouring syrups are obtainable from specialist outlets and are ideal for sweet-making as they are very concentrated.

SUGAR – ITS PROPERTIES

Sugar is the major ingredient in all confections. How it is treated in solution (ie. the sugar syrup) causes its transformation into the variety of textures that characterize different sweets – from the sparkling and glassy appearance of clear mints and lollipops to the soft crystalline texture of fudge and fondant.

When sugar is completely dissolved in water, it becomes a 'syrup'. Cold water will dissolve one and a half times its own weight of sugar, but when hot water is used it will absorb up to four times its weight. Beyond this, no more sugar can be absorbed.

As the syrup boils, so the water is driven off as steam, and the temperature of the syrup rises. The final temperature to which the syrup is allowed to rise controls the finished texture of the sweet. The more water that is driven off, the higher the sugar content, the higher the temperature and the harder the finished set.

TEMPERATURE AND TEXTURE CHART

The comparison between temperature and texture can be shown as follows:

Caramel	160 – 177°C 320 – 350°F	The syrup will have become honey to amber coloured. Above this temperature, it will taste bitter.
Hard Crack	149 – 154°C 300 – 310°F	Drop a little of the syrup into iced water. It will set and snap when bent. *(Butterscotch, Barley Sugar, Lollipops)*
Soft Crack	132 – 143°C 270 – 285°F	A little dropped into iced water will form hard but slightly elastic strands when stretched. *(Hard Caramels, Humbugs, Treacle Toffee)*
Hard Ball	121 – 130°C 250 – 266°F	After cooling, the syrup can be easily formed into a ball which will hold its shape. *(Nougat, Marshmallow)*
Firm Ball	118 – 121°C 244 – 250°F	Similar to *Hard Ball* but the ball will be more pliable and will quite quickly lose its shape. *(Caramels)*
Soft Ball	112 – 116°C 234 – 240°F	The syrup will form a ball in the iced water but will rapidly lose its shape when taken from the water and squeezed between the fingers. *(Fondant, Fudge)*
Thread	106 – 113°C 223 – 236°F	Dip the thumb and finger into cold water, then very quickly into the syrup, and again into cold water. Separate finger and thumb, and a thin thread of syrup will form.
Boiling	102 – 108°C 215 – 225°F	Sugar syrup boils
	100°C / 212°F	Water boils

GRAINING

As the water is driven off by boiling, so the sugar solution will try to crystallize or 'grain'. The successful sweet-maker will need to know how to make use of this graining tendency, both to discourage and encourage it as needed.

1. **To discourage graining**, an 'interfering agent' or 'doctor' must be added to the solution. These agents fall into two groups – food acids and the more commonly used sugar substances which do not crystallize easily.

   (a) **Food acids.** Acetic acid (found in vinegar); citric acid (from citrus fruits); tartaric acid (from grapes); and cream of tartar.

   (b) **Sugar substances.** Liquid and powdered glucose. Glucose has the added advantage in fondant and fudge – it helps to keep them moist and chewy.

   (c) **Brown sugar, golden syrup, treacle and honey** have some anti-graining properties, but they are variable and the effect can be unpredictable. They are more usually included for their flavouring properties.

   (d) **Milk solids and fats** also deter graining, particularly in caramels.

2. **To encourage graining**, there are two methods that may be used:

   (a) **Agitation** is employed after the syrup has boiled to its required temperature and then cooled slightly. The syrup is then beaten or 'turned' until a very slight grittiness can be detected and the mixture becomes cloudy or, in the case of fondant, it solidifies. If the syrup is beaten while still hot, the crystalline texture will be coarse. Beating the slightly cooled syrup produces a finer, smoother texture.

   (b) **Seeding** is simpler for the inexperienced sweet-maker and involves stirring a crystalline substance, such as a small quantity (approx. one rounded tbsp) of well-sifted icing sugar into the mixture when it reaches the required temperature. The finished sweet will assume the texture of the added sugar. For an even smoother texture, a small quantity of fondant, about 25 g (1 oz) (see recipe, pages 13/14) can be substituted for the icing sugar. When used in making fudge, this produces a particularly smooth and velvety texture.

From the above, it will be readily understood why it is essential in sweet-making that all the sugar should be completely dissolved before the syrup is allowed to boil; that any crystals that form on the sides of the pan during boiling should be washed off with a pastry brush; and that it is vital not to stir a boiling syrup unless the recipe specifically requires it.

HINTS FOR SUCCESS

1. **Read the recipe carefully** before you begin, and have all the necessary ingredients weighed and ready to hand. If ingredients such as liquid glucose, syrup and treacle are given by weight, weigh the sugar in the scale pan first, then add the syrup, etc. to this, then transfer both together to the pan.

2. **Prepare the tins, moulds or surfaces** for setting the mixture by lining with paper or oiling as necessary.

3. **Have to hand the pastry brush and a jug of hot water** containing the thermometer, if used. A cold thermometer may shatter if immersed directly into boiling syrup.

4. **Dissolve the sugar completely,** stirring with a metal spoon or spatula with an insulated handle. (A wooden one may discolour the syrup.) When the sugar is fully dissolved, the lid may be placed on the pan for the first minute or two of boiling, so that the steam which forms will wash down any stray crystals. Do not stir during the boiling unless the mixture contains milk or butter, in which case very gentle stirring is needed to prevent burning.

5. **When taking a thermometer reading,** make sure the bulb is completely immersed and the reading is taken at eye level. Remove the pan from the heat when checking and, when the required temperature is reached, dip the base of the pan into cold water to prevent further rise in temperature.

6. **Adding colour and flavour.** These should be carefully dripped from a teaspoon or skewer. Overdoing can spell ruin.

7. **Pouring out.** Do not attempt to scrape the pan clean. Cooled scrapings can already be starting to grain and could spoil the finished texture. However, where grain is required, the scrapings will assist the process.

8. **Mark the mixture** when it is almost set with an oiled knife. When totally cooled, the slab may then be broken up into pieces by tapping on the back.

9. **Finished sweets** should be stored in screw-topped jars or airtight tins, or wrapped in cellophane.

These hints will not be repeated in the recipes.

FONDANT

Fondant is a firm, white sugar paste which is the basis for the sweets known as 'Creams'. Its name translated from the French means 'melting' and appropriately describes its velvety texture. It has many uses in confectionery, from flavoured creams to coatings for nuts and fruits, and for stuffing dried fruits.

True home-made fondant is superior in taste and texture to any available substitute, and is well worth the effort involved in making it yourself, though it is not difficult.

Notes:
(a) If all the following methods seem rather daunting, there are other methods of producing acceptable creams. The cake covering sold in supermarkets and sugarcraft outlets, and known as 'Fondant Icing', makes a good substitute for cooked fondant and can be very successfully coloured, flavoured and shaped into very pleasant creams. Some confectioners also sell a fondant in powder form which has instructions for use included.

(b) Creams made from icing sugar alone, whether mixed with water or **egg albumen***, are the simplest of all to make. Children love to make these but they are intended to be eaten immediately as they dry out very quickly and become hard and brittle. They are also somewhat 'gritty', not velvety in texture. These disadvantages can be somewhat mitigated by the addition of powdered glucose, three parts icing sugar to one part of glucose.

***Egg albumen.** Use dried, pasteurised albumen, sold in supermarkets as 'Easy Egg White', reconstituted as directed. Do not use raw egg white.

As well as the usual equipment required for sugar boiling, you will need a surface on which to pour and work the syrup. Ideally this would be a marble slab, because of its firmness and coolness; if you are lucky enough to be able to acquire the top of an old washstand, this would be perfect. Marble slabs are obtainable from good kitchenware shops but can be expensive. One about 35 cm (14 ins) square is adequate. However, the normal formica or melamine kitchen work surface is quite suitable, since the temperature of the poured syrup will not be sufficiently high to damage it.

Also essential is a strong metal or wooden spatula with which to turn the syrup. An ideal tool for this can be the implement used to scrape wallpaper from the wall but, needless to say, NOT one that has been used for this purpose but one kept solely for culinary use. Care must be taken though, if using this on a work surface, as its sharp corners can cause damage by scoring if not handled with care.

BASIC FONDANT

Prepare the work surface by sprinkling lightly with cold water.

400 g (14 oz) granulated sugar
55 g (2 oz) powdered glucose
100 ml (3¹/₂ fl oz) water

1. Follow rules for sugar boiling (pages 9–11) and cook the syrup to 116°C/240°F.
2. Check the boil and pour the syrup on to the dampened slab or dish. Do not scrape the pan as this may cause unwanted crystals to form. Sprinkle a little more cold water over the surface of the syrup and leave until just warm, below 66°C/150°F. This should take about 10–15 minutes.
3. With the spatula or scraper, gather the outer edges of the pool of syrup and turn them into the centre. Keep working in this way in a 'figure of eight' movement. The syrup will become silvery, then thick and opaque, and will suddenly turn hard and crumble and pure white.
4. Leave to rest for about 15 minutes, covered with a clean, lightly dampened cloth.
5. Now scrape together all the crumble pieces and knead them together until the mixture becomes free of lumps and is then a smooth velvety paste.
6. The fondant needs to rest for one or two days to 'ripen' before it is ready for use, and should be stored in an airtight container in the refrigerator, where it will keep almost indefinitely.
7. This recipe makes approx. 450 g (1 lb) of fondant.

FONDANT – MAKING THE SWEETS

Starch Tray.

The professional method of making fondant creams involves melting the fondant and then pouring it into depressions made by moulds pressed into a tray of cornflour. This is known as a starch tray. If you intend to produce fondant sweets in quantity, it is possible for someone with a little craft skill to construct the tray and model the moulds needed.

The fondants set quickly in a starch tray; the cornflour assists in the drying out and helps to form a crust on the sweet's surface. The resulting sweets are very easily lifted from the starch.

Fondant Mat.

This is an alternative. It is made from solid rubber incorporating different shaped impressions into which the melted fondant is poured – no greasing or dusting is required. These mats are obtainable from specialist kitchenware shops. The sweets set within a minute or two and are released smooth and dry by twisting and bending the rubber mat. Fondant mats are expensive but worthwhile for the variety of shapes they can produce if you are making in quantity. Once purchased, fondant mats last a lifetime.

If you do not have the use of a starch tray or fondant mat, there are two other ways of forming the sweets:

Non-Melting Method.

If the fondant is firm, it can be coloured and flavoured and rolled out on to a board well-dusted with an equal mixture of sifted icing sugar and cornflour. The shapes can be cut with mini-cutters, available from kitchenware shops, or can be moulded in the hands. They should then be left to crust over on a tray well-dusted with the icing sugar and cornflour mixture. If the fondant seems to be rather soft, it can be firmed by the addition of sifted icing sugar.

Melting Method.

Large quantities of fondant should be melted in a bowl placed over a pan of hot water or by using a double saucepan but small quantities can be melted over direct heat with a little care. Working in small quantities I have found to be preferable, since the fondant sets so quickly that it is difficult to keep it warm and liquid for any length of time. Re-heated fondant quickly turns sugary and the distinctive texture is spoilt. Moreover, if you are making up a box of assorted sweets, then you will only need a few creams.

TO PRODUCE APPROX. 5–6 CREAMS

1. In a very small saucepan, place about 55 g (2 oz) of fondant (a quantity about the size of a golf ball). Add the desired colourings and flavourings. Be very sparing with the quantities here, as too much can over-thin this amount of fondant. When making PEPPERMINT CREAMS (p.18), one or at most two drops of oil of peppermint will be sufficient. If the fondant is very firm, it can be thinned by the addition of about 15 ml (1 tbsp) of stock syrup. This can be made by dissolving two parts of granulated sugar in one part of water and heating to 112°C/234°F.
2. Heat and stir very gently until the fondant is liquid and the colour and flavour incorporated. Remove from the heat if any bubbles appear. The fondant is ready to pour if, on tilting the pan, a slight wrinkling appears on the surface of the mixture.
3. Pour at once into the moulds, if you are using them, and leave to set. This should take about 3–5 minutes. Alternatively, drop teaspoonfuls on to a cornflour-dusted tray.

MINT CREAMS

1 packet of fondant
small amount of icing sugar
green colouring
small plastic round or half moon plastic or metal cutters
greaseproof paper
5–7 drops peppermint oil

1. Knead the fondant, adding a little peppermint oil at a time to get to the flavour required.
2. When the oil has been kneaded in, divide the fondant in half, colour one half with a little green colouring, not too bright, and knead in.
3. Roll out on a little icing sugar to 5 mm (¼ inch) thick and cut into shapes. Place on greaseproof paper to dry. The other half may be left white; roll out as above and cut into shape.

Notes:
(a) Oil of peppermint gives the best flavour. To ensure accuracy, measure the oil with a dropper.
(b) Peppermint essence does not give a true flavour. More essence than oil is needed and this may make the fondant or mixture too wet.

COFFEE CREAMS

110g (4 oz) cooked fondant
15 ml (1 tbsp) instant coffee powder
15 ml (1 tbsp) hot water

1. Place the fondant in a bowl over a pan of boiling water. Warm gently. Do not allow the temperature to rise above 60°C/140°F.
2. Dissolve the coffee in the hot water and stir into the fondant.
3. Pour into moulds using a spoon. Allow to set for several hours.
4. Turn out of moulds and dry on a wire rack before packing or dipping.

SUGAR FONDANT MICE

Use a packet of fondant icing and follow the instructions, or use the cooked fondant (page 14), or use the recipe below.

450 g (1 lb) icing sugar   **10 ml (2 tsp) cornflour**
Egg albumen equiv. to 1 egg white   **food colouring (pale pink)**
55 g (2 oz) golden syrup   **silver balls**

1. Beat together 225 g (8 oz) icing sugar, egg albumen and syrup into a bowl until smooth.
2. Gradually add the rest of the icing sugar and knead on a surface dusted with cornflour.
3. Divide the mixture in half and colour one half with pale pink colouring, leave the rest white. Keep covered with clingfilm to avoid drying out.
4. Take a piece of fondant about the size of a plum and form into a mouse with pointed nose. To make the ears, roll a small piece, the size of a pea, flatten and press into position on the head. Add two silver balls for eyes and make a tail by rolling a piece of fondant between the fingers and push in at the base of the back.

   Alternatively: *tails can be made of clean string or liquorice bootlaces; ears can be flaked almonds; eyes can be a dab of melted chocolate or gravy browning.*

5. Place on a sheet of non-stick paper, cover with another sheet and leave to set for approx. 2 days.

   Note: When using egg albumen, follow the manufacturer's instructions.

DOLLY MIXTURES

An alternative for MINT CREAMS (above).

1. Use a packet of fondant.
2. Colour $^1/_3$ pink, $^1/_3$ green.
3. Roll white, pink and green fondant $^1/_2$ cm ($^1/_4$ inch) thick.
4. Brush surface lightly with egg albumen.
5. Layer together.
6. Cut into dolly mixtures 2 cm ($^3/_4$ inch) square.

EASY UNCOOKED FONDANT

This is another uncooked fondant that works well.

225 g (8 oz) icing sugar
30 ml (2 tbsp) evaporated milk

1. Knead well together, colour and flavour as required.
2. Must be kept in refrigerator or eaten immediately.

PEPPERMINT CREAMS

This is a recipe, without eggs, from 1896, from Vogehers' *Cookery Recipe Book*, which cost 3 old pence. It was my grandmother's. Originally, the weights were in cups and spoons.

225 g (8 oz) icing sugar
25 g (1 oz) potatoes (peeled, boiled and sieved to a smooth consistency)
peppermint flavouring, or peppermint oil to taste
green colouring
110 g (4 oz) chocolate for covering, melted in a bowl over warm water

1. Beat the potatoes and icing sugar together, or use a liquidizer.
2. Add the flavouring to taste and a little green colouring.
3. Form into balls. Either flatten slightly and dip only half in chocolate and place on foil to dry – or make into balls and dip all in chocolate and place on foil to dry.

FUDGE

Fudge is recognized by its distinctive texture – soft, moist and chewy. It is, in effect, a caramel cooked to slightly lower temperature, to achieve a softer result, and then encouraged to 'grain' (page 11 – SUGAR AND ITS PROPERTIES). In fact, the story goes that fudge originated by chance, when a mixture intended to be a caramel was accidentally beaten.

VANILLA FUDGE

225 g (8 oz) granulated sugar
110 g (4 oz) powdered glucose
175 g (6 oz) condensed milk
55 g (2 oz) unsalted or lightly salted butter
vanilla flavouring (approx. $^1/_2$ tsp)
150 ml ($^1/_4$ pint water)

1. Follow the method for CARAMELS (page 28), warming the butter and milk together separately, but boil the sugar syrup to 116°C/240°F, soft ball.
2. After the addition of the combined milk and butter, stir the boiling mixture very gently until the temperature returns to the soft ball stage. The mixture at this stage should be a light golden brown. For a slightly firmer fudge, the mixture may be boiled to 121°C/250°F.
3. Remove the pan from the heat and check the boil. Beat the mixture well with a wooden spoon or spatula until it loses its gloss and becomes cloudy. A slight 'grittiness' can be felt when rubbing the spoon against the sides of the pan, indicating that 'graining' is beginning.

4. Stir in the vanilla flavouring and pour the mixture into the prepared tin, scraping all the mixture from the pan and the spoon. These last vestiges will be graining rapidly as they cool and will encourage the total poured mix to grain.

5. Cool, then mark into squares or bite-sized pieces with a greased knife. This quantity will make a slab approx. 20 x 15 cm (8 x 6 ins) and 1 cm ($^1/_2$ inch) deep.

6. If you are unsure of exactly how much beating is necessary to encourage 'graining', use the 'seeding' method described in the section SUGAR – ITS PROPERTIES, page 11). The mixture may look more like a caramel as it is poured but it will grain as it cools and sets. Confidence in knowing the extent of beating necessary does come with practice.

VARIATIONS:

CHOCOLATE FUDGE
Add 55 g (2 oz) chopped or melted chocolate before beating.

RUM FUDGE
Omit the vanilla flavouring and add rum flavouring before beating.

NUT/FRUIT FUDGE
Warm 55 g (2 oz) chopped nuts or sultanas, currants, dates, chopped glacé cherries, preserved ginger, or a mixture of these, and stir into the mixture after beating. Alternatively, nuts can be sprinkled on to the mixture after it is poured and pressed in with a spatula or rolling pin.

COFFEE FUDGE
If using coffee essence or dissolved instant coffee (approx 2 tsp), the mixture should be cooked slightly harder to 118°C/244°F to compensate for the addition of the extra liquid.

MARSHMALLOW
Add 175 g (6 oz) chopped marshmallows to mixture before beating.

HONEY FUDGE
Cook the mixture to 118°C/244°F. Add 2 or 3 tsp of honey after the graining has been achieved. Do not add the honey before beating, since the honey itself, being a 'doctoring agent' (see SUGAR section, page 11) would act to inhibit graining.

CANDIES

Candy is harder and has a much coarser grained texture than fudge; the sugar crystals are very obvious in the finished product. In effect, if fudge is overbeaten, it will turn to candy.

The tastiest candies are those that are fruit-flavoured. However, fruit juices tend to be too thin to impart sufficient flavour and are not generally to be recommended for sweet-making. Orange and lemon flavours are extracted from the 'zest' of these fruits, not the juice. There are, however, some excellent concentrated fruit juices – orange, lemon and grapefruit – to be found in frozen food outlets; these are ideal for making candies. Fresh or frozen fruits may also be used by heating them gently until the juices run, then straining.

Less glucose is included in candy recipes, since a coarser grain than that of fudge is to be desired. Fat is not included in fruit candies.

ORANGE OR LEMON CANDY

This makes a slab of candy approx. 13 x 13 cm (5 x 5 ins) square by approx. 2 cm ($^3/_4$ ins) deep.

350 g (12 oz) granulated sugar
25 g (1 oz) powdered glucose
100 ml ($3^1/_2$ fl oz) water
30 ml (2 tbsp) concentrated fruit juice
5 ml (1 tsp) grated orange or lemon zest
1 pinch ($^1/_4$ tsp) citric acid, dissolved in a little water
10 ml (2 tsp) icing sugar

1. Follow the rules for sugar boiling (pages 9–11), dissolving the sugar and glucose in the water.
2. Boil the syrup to 121°C/250°F. Check the boil and add the remaining ingredients.
3. Stir to incorporate the icing sugar and pour into a tin lined with silicone paper. As the mixture cools, it will gradually 'grain', though it will appear quite liquid when poured.
4. When cool, cut into bite-sized pieces or squares.

PEPPERMINT CANDY (MINT CAKE)

Use the recipe on previous page for ORANGE OR LEMON CANDY, omitting the citric acid, fruit concentrate and grated peel. Add a few drops of oil of peppermint with the icing sugar. Peppermint candy may be coloured green if desired.

Note: The final temperature for peppermint candy can be 121°C/250°F only, since the syrup is not thinned by the addition of the extra liquid.

MUSCOVADO TABLET

150 ml (5 fl oz) single cream
25 g (1 oz) butter

450 g (1 lb) muscovado sugar
2.5 ml ($^1/_2$ tsp) vanilla essence

1. Place the cream, butter and sugar in a large pan and bring to the boil.
2. Bring to a temperature of 118°C/244°F, stirring all the time.
3. Remove from the heat, add the vanilla essence, and beat the mixture to thicken.
4. Pour into a greased 18 x 18 cm (7 x 7 ins) tin.
5. Mark into squares.

GOLDEN SPONGE CANDY

450 g (1 lb) brown sugar
150 ml ($^1/_4$ pint) water

5 ml (1 tsp) vanilla essence
5 ml (1 tsp) bicarbonate of soda

1. Using a large pan, dissolve the sugar in the water, then follow the rules for boiling sugar (pages 9–11).
2. Boil until a temperature of 121°C/250°F hard boil is reached.
3. Remove the pan from the heat.
4. Add the essence and bicarbonate of soda. Stir in. The candy will puff up in the pan.
5. Pour into an oiled tin 15 cm (6 ins) square.
6. Mark while hot and cut when cold.

Note: The candy is very crumbly. The crumb can be used as a topping for uncooked fruit cakes or puddings; eg. crumbles on ice cream, or folded into fresh cream and used as a filling.

NOUGAT & MARSHMALLOWS

Nougat and Marshmallows are created by combining the hot sugar syrup with a foam. This foam is made by beating egg whites or melted gelatine and is mixed with the boiling syrup when this reaches the required temperature.

Nougat can have the texture of a caramel, soft and chewy, or be grainy like a candy. The chewy kind is poured as soon as the foam is incorporated, whereas the candy type, which has less 'doctoring agent' (glucose) is beaten before pouring, to induce graining.

The foam produced by whisking egg whites gives a better flavour than gelatine but is slightly more difficult to use since it is less stable. Nougat made with egg white cannot be re-heated if it begins to set too soon, since it will begin to burn. Gelatine-based nougat can be re-heated successfully without the likelihood of it burning, and this is the preferred method for a more chewy nougat.

The procedure is to whisk the egg white until stiff, or begin to whisk the melted gelatine and, while continuing to whisk, slowly add the hot syrup and incorporate by continual whisking. This can easily be done if the whisking is carried out in an electric mixer, leaving the hands free to pour the syrup, but if working solely by hand, a helpful friend to pour the syrup can make the process much easier.

A basic nougat contains almonds, pistachios, cherries and angelica. Nougat Montelimar has added honey for extra flavour – since this itself is an invert sugar, less glucose can be used. Nuts, which must be skinned, and fruits must be warmed before added to the mixture (5 mins in the oven at 180°C/350°F/Gas 4), so that they do not cool the mixture and set it prematurely.

The flavour of hazelnuts and blanched almonds is improved by 'roasting' in a medium heat to a pale golden brown. Avoid over-browning, otherwise the nuts become bitter. Cook either in a heavy saucepan over a low heat or in an oven at a low temperature 130°C/250°F/Gas ½. After 'roasting' rub hazelnuts in a dry cloth to remove skins.

You will also need rice paper with which to coat the nougat and a suitable board and weights to keep the mixture under pressure when setting. Edible rice paper is obtainable from good stationers.

CHEWY NOUGAT

350 g (12 oz) granulated sugar
225 g (8 oz) powdered glucose
1 large egg, white only, or 40 g (1½ oz) albumen
    or **15 g (½ oz or 4 tsp) powdered gelatine soaked for 10 minutes in**
      30 ml (2 tbsp) cold water, then melted in a bowl placed over hot water.
450 g (1 lb) nuts and fruit – almonds, hazelnuts, cherries, etc.
rice paper

1. Following the rules for sugar boiling (pages 9–11), dissolve the sugar and glucose in 150 ml (5 fl oz) water and boil to 132°C/270°F.
2. While the syrup is boiling, whisk the egg white in a heat-proof bowl until it forms fairly stiff peaks. While still continuing to whisk, pour the hot syrup in a steady stream on to the egg whites, taking care not to let the syrup trickle down the side of the bowl or it will set hard there.
3. Alternatively begin to beat the melted gelatine, if using, and add the hot syrup in the same way, taking the same precautions not to allow the syrup to make contact with the sides of the bowl.
4. When the syrup is fully incorporated, stir in the warmed nuts and fruit. This quantity of mixture will hold up to 450 g (1 lb) of almonds, hazelnuts, cherries, or any combination of these.
5. Quickly pour the mixture into a tin lined with a sheet of rice paper. Press a second sheet of rice paper on the surface, place a board on top and weight this down. This quantity will make a slab about 25 x 18 cm (10 x 7 ins) and sufficient weight would be about 900 g (2 lb).
6. Leave under the weight for about 6 hours to set.
7. To divide the nougat into even-shaped pieces, remove the board after about 30 minutes and score the slab by pressing a sharp knife down about 5 mm (¼ inch). Replace the board and weights. Leave for the remaining time to set.

CANDY NOUGAT

450 g (1 lb) granulated sugar
110 g (4 oz) powdered glucose
1 large egg, white only, or 40 g (1½ oz) albumen
    or **15 g (½ oz) powdered gelatine soaked for 10 minutes in 30 ml (2 tbsp)**
    water, then melted in a bowl over hot water.

1. Follow the method for chewy nougat until the syrup has been fully incorporated, then beat the mixture with a metal spoon until it becomes slightly less glossy and begins to feel a little lumpy.
2. Add the desired nuts and fruit.
3. Finish as in the previous method for CHEWY NOUGAT (page 24).

GOLDEN NOUGAT

This is a very sweet chewy nougat.

450 g (1 lb) granulated sugar
150 ml (¼ pint) water
3 level tbsp golden syrup
pinch cream of tartar
3 tbsp honey

4 egg whites
110 g (4 oz) blanched pistachio nuts
few drops vanilla essence
rice paper or wafers

1. Dissolve the sugar in the water and boil until the mixture reaches 132°C/270°F, very firm ball.
2. Stir in cream of tartar.
3. While syrup is boiling, warm the honey separately. Whisk egg whites in big bowl until very stiff. While still continuing to whisk, pour on the syrup, avoiding the sides of the bowl. When thoroughly blended, add hot honey and chopped nuts and essence.
4. Line a 23–25 cm (9–10 ins) square tin with rice paper or wafers and pour over mixture. Cover with more wafers or paper and leave to set. Cut in pieces. Or put into oiled tin without wafers or rice paper. Wrap in waxed paper to prevent becoming sticky.

VARIATION:
Use the recipe above but omit golden syrup. This gives a firmer, whiter sweet.

NOUGAT MONTELIMAR

400 g (14 oz) granulated sugar
55 g (2 oz) powdered glucose
110 g (4 oz) clear honey
15 g (¹/₂ oz) powdered gelatine
    soaked in 30 ml (2 tbsp) water
    and melted in a bowl of hot water

225 g (8 oz) blanched almonds
175 g (6 oz) glacé cherries
55 g (2 oz) pistachio nuts or angelica,
                   chopped

1. Cook the syrup to 132°C/270°F, while warming the honey separately.
2. Add the honey to the syrup and boil to 135°C/275°F.
3. Pour the syrup gradually into the melted gelatine while beating the mixture vigorously.
4. Fold in the warmed nuts and fruit.
5. Finish as for CHEWY NOUGAT (page 24).

NOUGAT & MARZIPAN SQUARES

225 g (8 oz) caster sugar
1.25 ml (¹/₄ tsp) pure glycerine
10 ml (2 tsp) lemon juice
80 g (3 oz) blanched almonds, chopped

80 g (3 oz) glacé cherries, chopped
small qty marzipan or almond paste
rice paper (optional)

1. Using a strong saucepan, heat and stir the sugar, glycerine and lemon juice until the sugar has dissolved.
2. Cook until the mixture looks like syrup and is a pale biscuit colour.
3. Add the chopped almonds and cherries and mix well.
4. Turn out on a cool surface which has been slightly oiled or greased, and mould into a square
5. Alternatively, it can be poured into a tin lined with rice paper.
6. Allow to cool after marking into 2.5 cm (1 inch) squares.
7. While the nougat is cooling, roll the prepared marzipan or almond paste on a sugared board to approx. 5 mm (¹/₄ inch) and cut into 2.5 cm (1 inch) wide strips.
8. When the nougat is cold, roll a strip of almond paste around 4 sides and seal the joint firmly with a knife.
9. Roll in caster sugar.

LAYERED NOUGAT

1. Make any of the nougat recipes.
2. Pour half into a tin lined with rice paper and immediately colour the remainder a pale pink or very delicate green.
3. Pour on top of the white layer at once and allow to set.

MARSHMALLOWS
(makes about 450–525 g (1 lb – 19 oz)

275 g (10 oz) granulated sugar
10 ml (2 tsp) liquid glucose
150 ml (5 fl oz / $^{1}/_{4}$ pint) water
white of one egg
20 g ($^{3}/_{4}$ oz) powdered gelatine

150 ml (5 fl oz / $^{1}/_{4}$ pint) cold water mixed with 30 ml (2 tbsp) orange flower water.
25 g (1 oz) icing sugar and 25 g (1 oz) cornflour sifted together

1. Lightly oil a tin (approx. 25 x 20 cm / 10 x 8 ins) – and dust with a little of the cornflour/icing-sugar mixture.
2. Put the water/orange-flower-water mix into a large bowl (1.7 litre / 3 pint size) and sprinkle the powdered gelatine over it, then place the bowl over a pan of boiling water and stir occasionally to dissolve.
3. Whisk the egg white into stiff peaks.
4. Place the sugar, glucose and water in a saucepan. Follow the rules for sugar boiling (pages 9–11) and boil the syrup to 126°C/260°F. Remove from the heat and, while whisking steadily, pour the syrup on to the gelatine mixture.
5. Combine with the beaten egg white, still beating until the mixture becomes light and fluffy and will hold its shape, though still thin enough to flow.
6. Spread the mixture immediately into the prepared tin, smoothing with a palette knife. Leave to set for several hours.
7. Loosen the mixture from the sides of the tin. Dust the surface with remaining cornflour/icing-sugar mix and turn out the contents of the tin on to this.
8. Keeping all exposed surfaces of the marshmallow well dusted, cut into squares with an oiled knife or scissors, frequently wiping and re-oiling as necessary.
9. Making sure all cut surfaces are well coated with the cornflour/icing-sugar mix, dry the pieces on a wire rack for a few hours.
10. Store in an airtight container lined with greaseproof or waxed paper. They will keep for about 2 weeks.

Note: By using two separate tins to set the mixture, the second half may be tinted pink before pouring.

CARAMELS, TOFFEES & BUTTERSCOTCH

Caramels, Toffees and Butterscotch can all be made from the same basic recipe. The difference is in the final temperature to which the mixture is cooked.

Caramels: 118–121°C/244–250°F is adequate. Gives a moist, chewy texture.
Toffee: 132–143°C/270–285°F gives a hard texture.
Butterscotch: 149–154°C/300–310°F gives the characteristic brittleness.

Careful attention to temperature is essential. For good results, it is advisable to use a sugar thermometer.

Caramels have a firm texture and last a long time; however, they are much enjoyed by all ages, and so, if you leave them lying around, they may not last as long as you hoped!

Notes on Caramels:
(a) Caramels can be coated with chocolate.
(b) A temperature of 1 or 2 degrees higher should be used when making caramels in very hot weather, so that they will harden.
(c) Store in airtight tins.
(d) Caramels can be made in fairly large quantities. They keep well.

CARAMEL (1)

450 g (1 lb) granulated sugar
110 g (4 oz) powdered glucose
25 g (1 oz) unsalted butter

150 ml (¼ pint) water
150 ml (¼ pint) single cream

1. Oil an 18 cm (7 ins) square tin.
2. Mix together the sugar and water in a heavy-based saucepan. Heat gently to dissolve the sugar. Stir all the time.
3. Stir in the glucose and bring to the boil. Do not stir. Allow temperature to rise to 121°C/250°F.
4. Gently heat together the cream and butter.
5. Add this to the syrup when the temperature is reached. Lower the temperature. Stir gently and allow temperature to return to 121°C/250°F.
6. Pour into the prepared tin. Leave to cool.
7. Turn out of tin when firm enough to handle. Cut into pieces with scissors.

CARAMEL (2)

225 g (8 oz) granulated sugar
110 g (4 oz) powdered glucose
175 g (6 oz) condensed milk
55 g (2 oz) butter
vanilla flavouring

1. Dissolve the sugar and glucose in 150 ml (¼ pint) water.
2. Place milk and butter in a small pan, and warm gently to melt the butter and combine it with the milk.
3. Boil the sugar syrup to 121°C/250°F firm ball. Add warmed butter and milk slowly, lower the heat and bring mixture back to the boil. Stir very gently with a wooden spatula, to prevent the mixture from burning. Boil to 126°C/260°F.
4. Remove pan from heat. Dip the base into cold water to prevent further cooking. Gently stir in a little vanilla flavouring if required. Pour into prepared tin to set.
5. When nearly set, mark into bite-sized pieces.

Note: For a more chewy caramel, use 225 g (8 oz) glucose. For a much richer caramel, increase the quantity of condensed milk to 275 g (10 oz).

CHOCOLATE CARAMELS
Add 55 g (2 oz) chopped chocolate and stir in gently just before pouring.

COFFEE CARAMELS
Omit vanilla flavouring. Gently stir in 15 ml (1 tbsp) coffee essence or strong dissolved instant coffee just before pouring. This small quantity of extra liquid tends to soften the mixture, so final pouring temperature should be 130°C/266°F.

NUT CARAMELS
Add 55 g (2 oz) of warmed, chopped nuts just before pouring.

FRUIT CARAMELS
Add 55 g (2 oz) warmed currants, sultanas, dates, cherries, or any combination of these just before pouring.

GINGER CARAMELS
Add 110 g (4 oz) chopped crystallized ginger just before the right temperature.

COCONUT CARAMELS
Add 110 g (4 oz) coconut to the mixture just before pouring.

TOFFEES

These are possibly one of the greatest favourites with most people, and are simple to make. Toffees may be coated with chocolate. When not coated with chocolate, they should be individually wrapped in waxed paper. The basic CARAMEL recipe can be used for plain toffee but the mixture should be cooked to a final temperature of 138°C/280° F.

RICH TREACLE TOFFEE

110 g (4 oz) granulated sugar	**110 g (4 oz) powdered glucose**
110 g (4 oz) brown sugar	**80 g (3 oz) butter**
80 g (3 oz) black treacle	**5 ml (1 tsp) lemon juice**

1. Dissolve the sugars and glucose in 150 ml (¼ pint) water.
2. Gently warm the butter in a separate pan until just melted.
3. Boil the sugar syrup to 130°C/266°F, then add the butter and treacle and bring the mixture back to the boil and cook to a final temperature of 132–135°C/270–275°F.
4. Prevent further cooking by dipping the base of the pan into cold water, add the lemon juice and pour into the prepared tin.

   ALTERNATIVE:
   For a creamier toffee, warm 175 g (6 oz) condensed milk with only 55 g (2 oz) of the butter. The addition of the milk in this way may produce a curdled appearance in the cooking. This is caused by the acids in the treacle and brown sugar, but it is not apparent in the finished toffee.

TREACLE TOFFEE (1)

450 g (1 lb) soft brown sugar
1.25 ml (¼ level tsp) cream of tartar
80 g (3 oz) butter

110 g (4 oz) golden syrup
150 ml (¼ pint) water
110 g (4 oz) black treacle

1. Dissolve the sugar in the water in a large, heavy-based saucepan over a low heat.
2. Add the remaining ingredients and bring to the boil. Boil to 132–143°C/270–285°F soft crack stage. Stir gently to prevent burning. Check temperature rise.
3. Pour into a 30 x 10 cm (12 x 4 ins) greased tin. Cool for 5 minutes and, when beginning to set, mark into squares.
4. Leave until cold and break up.
5. Wrap in waxed paper and store in jars or airtight tins.
6. Makes 800 g (1¾ lb).

TOFFEE APPLES

450 g (1 lb) demerara sugar
10 ml (2 tsp) vinegar
15 ml (1 level tbsp) golden syrup
55 g (2 oz) butter

150 ml (¼ pint) water
6–8 medium-sized sweet apples
same number of wooden sticks

1. Place the sugar, butter, vinegar, water and syrup in a heavy-based saucepan and heat the mixture gently. When the sugar has dissolved, boil the mixture rapidly for 5 minutes until the temperature reaches 132–143°C/270–285°F soft crack stage.
2. Wipe the apples and push the sticks into the cores. Dip the apples into the toffee, and then twirl around for a few seconds to allow the excess toffee to drip off.
3. Leave to cool and set on a buttered baking sheet or waxed paper.

The following toffee recipes, it will be noted, have minimal quantities of water and therefore the rule regarding the complete dissolving of the sugar before boiling cannot be followed. However, the sugar crystals will dissolve, but as very little moisture needs to be driven off in the boiling process the final temperature will be reached very quickly, particularly after it reaches 121°C/250°F, so the thermometer must be very carefully watched.

GOLDEN SYRUP TOFFEE

450 g (1 lb) sugar
175 g (6 oz) golden syrup
55 g (2 oz) butter

15 ml (1 tbsp) vinegar
15 ml (1 tbsp) water

1. Put all the ingredients into the pan, stir gently and bring to the boil. Cook to 143°C/290°F.
2. Pour into prepared tin and mark into squares just before completely cold.

VARIATIONS:
To the GOLDEN TOFFEE recipe add:
150 g (5 oz) chopped walnuts, hazelnuts, almonds or Brazils
or 110 g (4 oz) chopped dates, cherries or raisins
or 7 drops oil of peppermint – add just before mixture reaches the hard crack stage.

NUT TOFFEE

As GOLDEN SYRUP TOFFEE but sprinkle 110 g (4 oz) chopped walnuts, almonds or Brazils over the base of the prepared tin before pouring the syrup.

CHOCOLATE COATED TOFFEE

As GOLDEN SYRUP TOFFEE but sprinkle with 225 g (8 oz) grated chocolate; this will melt on the hot toffee. Re-mark squares.

TREACLE TOFFEE (2)

175 g (6 oz) soft brown sugar
110 g (4 oz) black treacle
110 g (4 oz) butter

45 ml (3 tbsp) water
1.25 ml ($1/4$ tsp) cream of tartar

1. Combine sugar, treacle, butter and water in the pan.
2. Add the cream of tartar. Boil to 126°C/260°F, stirring carefully to prevent burning.
3. Check the boil and pour into prepared tin.
4. Mark into pieces before completely set.

BUTTERSCOTCH

Butterscotch is delicious to eat and not difficult to make. It is used as a sweet by itself or in a similar form with nuts. Since the sweetmeats are generally large when nuts have been coated, you do not use them with chocolate. The very high temperature to which butterscotch is boiled makes it essential to use a strong pan. Wrap individual sweets in waxed paper, and store in a tin.

450 g (1 lb) demerara sugar
55 g (2 oz) butter
150 ml (¹/₄ pint) water

1. Dissolve the sugar in the water and bring to the boil. Boil, without stirring, until temperature reaches 138°C/280°F.
2. Add the butter cut into small pieces and continue boiling to 149°C/300°F.
3. Pour into prepared tin and mark into pieces when almost set.
4. Makes approx. 450 g (1 lb)

   VARIATION:
   Substitute 225 g (8 oz) granulated sugar and 80 g (3 oz) powdered glucose for the demerara sugar and add a little lemon flavouring just before pouring.

BUTTERED BRAZILS

225 g (8 oz) granulated sugar **150 ml (¹/₄ pint) water**
175 g (6 oz) powdered glucose **16 Brazil nuts**
55 g (2 oz) butter

1. Follow the recipe for BUTTERSCOTCH above. The glucose is necessary to avoid the risk of graining, as the dipping of the nuts involves a certain amount of agitation.
2. Do not pour out the mixture but keep it warm enough to remain liquid.
3. Drop the skinned nuts into the mixture. Lift out on a fork and drop on to an oiled surface to set.
4. Almonds and walnuts may be substituted.

   Note: When the mixture becomes too cloudy and stiff, turn out and allow to cool. Crush, and store in an airtight jar and use to sprinkle on the surface of fruit cakes, etc., before baking, or on tray bakes instead of icing sugar.

BOILED SWEETS & LOLLIPOPS

Fruit drops are the easiest of the boiled sweets and are made by boiling a sugar syrup to the 'hard crack' stage, 149°C/300°F, then spooning it in small pools on to a cold, oiled surface – a marble slab is excellent, or baking sheet. By adding a paper or wooden stick while the pool is still liquid, the sweet becomes a lollipop.

Synthetic flavourings and colourings may be used but the most tempting sweets incorporate fresh fruit juices. These can be used in the form of the frozen concentrated citrus fruit juices or by warming soft fruits gently until the juice flows, then straining this off and incorporating the clear juice in the recipe. Flavouring extracts should be added to the boiled syrup after the required setting point is reached.

CLEAR FRUIT DROPS & LOLLIPOPS

225 g (8 oz) granulated sugar   10 ml (2 tsp) liquid glucose
few drops flavouring and colouring   80 ml (3 fl oz) water
     eg. raspberry + cochineal; lemon + yellow colouring;
     2–3 drops oil of peppermint + green colouring

1. Follow the rules for sugar boiling (pages 9–11) and heat the syrup to 148°C/298°F. Boil to 149°C/300°F. Add flavouring and colouring.
2. Remove from heat. Do not check the boil, as the mixture sets very quickly.
3. Pour into an oiled tin or spoon in individual shapes on to an oiled slab.
4. If in the tin, mark immediately into squares and, when cooled, break into pieces. Wrap the pieces or drops in cellophane.
5. Lollipops should also be wrapped but can be made extra tempting by sealing them in a bag of sherbert to make the old-fashioned 'Sherbert Dabs'.

SHERBERT

110 g (4 oz) icing sugar   15–20 ml (3–4 tsp) tartaric acid
5 ml (1 tsp) bicarbonate of soda

1. Sieve all the ingredients together twice.
2. Makes about 200 ml (13 tbsp). One tablespoon is sufficient for each lollipop.

BARLEY SUGAR TWISTS

450 g (1 lb) granulated sugar   juice of $\frac{1}{2}$ lemon
150 ml ($\frac{1}{4}$ pint) water   pinch cream of tartar

1. Follow rules for sugar boiling (pages 9–11) and dissolve sugar in the water.
2. Stir in the cream of tartar and boil the syrup to 116°C/240°F.
3. Add the lemon juice and continue boiling to 154°C/310°F, hard crack stage.
4. Pour the mixture on to a lightly oiled slab or baking sheet.
5. Leave until cool enough to handle, then with oiled hands lift the two longer sides to the middle.
6. With oiled scissors, cut across the folds into strips, working from the ends to the middle; ie. handling the more rapidly cooling sections first.
7. Twist each strip into a corkscrew shape. The twists should be kept in an airtight container or wrapped individually in cellophane.
8. Makes about 450 g (1 lb) sweets.

PULLED TOFFEE
An alternative to BARLEY SUGAR TWISTS (above). The method is similar.

675 g (1$\frac{1}{2}$ lb) granulated sugar   5 ml (1 tsp) vanilla essence
75 ml (2$\frac{1}{2}$ fl oz) vinegar   150 ml (5 fl oz) water
15 g ($\frac{1}{2}$ oz) butter

1. Put vinegar, water and sugar into a clean pan. Boil for 15 minutes.
2. Add butter, cut up, and boil for another 15 minutes.
3. Turn out toffee on to greased plate. Sprinkle vanilla essence.
4. When cool enough to handle, with oiled hands turn edges inward, hang mixture up, pull lengthways, hang again, repeat until streaked with white.
5. Twist in sticks about 2 cm ($\frac{3}{4}$ inch) thick. Cut into 1 and 2.5 cm ($\frac{1}{2}$ and 1 inch) lengths. Put on greased paper to set.

ACID DROPS

450 g (1 lb) granulated sugar
125 ml (4 fl oz) water
pinch of cream of tartar

2 or 3 drops lemon essence
5 ml (1 tsp) tartaric acid

1. Dissolve the sugar and cream of tartar in the water and boil the syrup to 154°C/310°F.
2. Add the tartaric acid, dissolved in a little warm water.
3. Allow to cool slightly until starting to thicken, then pour small drops from an oiled teaspoon on to an oiled surface.
4. Wrap in cellophane when cool.

MINT HUMBUGS

450 g (1 lb) demerara sugar
150 ml (¼ pint) water
55 g (2 oz) butter

pinch cream of tartar
few drops oil of peppermint

1. Put sugar, water, butter and cream of tartar into a saucepan and boil to the soft crack stage, 143°C/290°F.
2. Allow to cool for a minute in the pan. Add oil of peppermint and pour on to an oiled slab.
3. Pull into long strips and cut into pieces.
4. Leave until cool enough to handle, then with oiled hands lift the two longer sides to the middle, as with BARLEY SUGAR TWISTS above.
5. With oiled scissors, cut across the folds into strips, working from the ends to the middle; ie. handling the more rapidly cooling sections first.
6. Store in an airtight container.

SHADED MINT HUMBUGS

1. Use the recipe for mint humbugs but pull half of the mixture rather more vigorously, so it is a little paler in colour.
2. Put the pale strip and the dark strip together and roll up so you have a slightly striped effect.
3. Cut into pieces.
4. Store in an airtight tin.

TURKISH DELIGHT

Three rather different recipes follow. Traditional Turkish Delight uses a specially treated form of starch to produce the set – this is usually only available to the trade. Agar, a substance derived from seaweed, can be used and is readily available in health food shops. It does have the advantage of being suitable for vegetarians. Setting produced by the use of gelatine is cheaper and more easily obtainable. It is possible to use some of these in combination, as in the third recipe. Cornflour, the starch element, is included to thicken the mixture and gelatine provides the final set. Gelatine used on its own produces a more rubbery texture. Cornflour on its own gives a more traditional jelly consistency.

TURKISH DELIGHT (1)

450 g (1 lb) granulated sugar
25 g (1 oz) powdered gelatine
275 ml ($^1/_2$ pint) cold water

1 orange, rind and juice
1 lemon, juice only
Cornflour and icing sugar for dusting

1. Prepare a tin, approx. 15 x 10 cm (6 x 4 ins) by sprinkling it with water.
2. Put 150 ml ($^1/_4$ pint) of the water into a small pan. Sprinkle gelatine over the surface. Place over gentle heat, stir until gelatine dissolves. Boil for 3–4 minutes.
3. In another pan, dissolve the sugar in the remaining water and bring to the boil. Allow to cool slightly. Add the gelatine mixture and simmer gently, stirring all the time, for 20 minutes. Remove from the heat.
4. Add the orange and lemon juices and the pared orange rind. Cover and leave to stand for 15–20 minutes.
5. Strain into the prepared tin and leave to set.
6. Cut into squares and toss in cornflour and then in sifted icing sugar.
7. Pack in an airtight box lined with waxed paper, making sure there is plenty of icing sugar to coat the pieces. This Turkish Delight keeps well.

TURKISH DELIGHT (2)

A little more difficult but the flavour is superior. The boiling time must not be shortened, as this prolonged cooking inhibits the tendency of the finished sweet to 'weep'. This does not keep as long as TURKISH DELIGHT (1).

450 g (1 lb) granulated sugar
850 ml (1½ pints) water
2.5 ml (½ tsp) tartaric acid
200 g (7 oz) sifted icing sugar

80 g (3 oz) cornflour
55 g (2 oz) honey
30 ml (2 tbsp) lemon juice or rose water
pink colouring, if using rosewater

1. Lightly oil a tin, approx. 18 x 13 cm (7 x 5 ins).
2. Dissolve the granulated sugar in 150 ml (¼ pint) of the water. Boil to 116°C/240°F. Stir in the tartaric acid and set aside.
3. Blend the icing sugar and cornflour with a little of the remaining water. Boil the rest of the water in a pan, then carefully stir in the icing sugar and cornflour mix, bring back to the boil and boil until thickened and clear.
4. Add prepared syrup and lemon juice, or rose water and colouring. Boil steadily for 25–30 minutes, stirring frequently until mixture is transparent. Remove from heat and stir in honey. Pour into prepared tin. Leave until cold and set.
5. Turn out and cut up, dusting pieces liberally with sifted icing sugar or sherbert (see page 35). Pack as in TURKISH DELIGHT (1).

LEMON TURKISH DELIGHT

15 g (½ oz) gelatine
2 lemons, zest and juice
450 g (1 lb) granulated sugar

55 g (2 oz) cornflour
water
icing sugar and cornflour for coating

1. Dissolve the gelatine in 50 ml (2 fl oz) water.
2. Put the lemon juice, zest, sugar and 100 ml (4 fl oz) water in a pan and heat until the sugar has dissolved. Boil to 112°C/234°F.
3. Strain. Return syrup to the pan.
4. Slake the cornflour with a little water and whisk into the syrup.
5. Gradually add the gelatine.
6. Bring the mixture back up to the boil. Stir to prevent burning.
7. Boil for 10 minutes.
8. Pour into a wet tin 20 cm (8 ins) square. Allow to set for 24 hours.
9. Cut into cubes and roll in a mixture of icing sugar and cornflour.
10. Store in an airtight container.

TURKISH DELIGHT (3)

275 g (10 oz) granulated sugar
25 g (1 oz) cornflour
15 g ($^1\!/_2$ oz) powdered gelatine
15 g ($^1\!/_2$ oz) liquid glucose
pinch of citric acid

juice of 1 orange and $^1\!/_2$ lemon
2.5 ml ($^1\!/_2$ tsp) flavouring (rum, vanilla,
   strawberry, raspberry)
colouring as appropriate

1. Line a tin with greaseproof paper.
2. Dissolve gelatine in 75 ml (2$^1\!/_2$ fl oz) water. Slake cornflour with a little water.
3. Following the rules for sugar boiling (pages 9–11), dissolve the sugar in 150 ml ($^1\!/_4$ pint) water and boil for 3 minutes.
4. Add the gelatine, cornflour, glucose and citric acid, and boil, stirring constantly, until the syrup begins to clear.
5. Add the fruit juices and continue boiling for about 5 minutes, by which time the mixture should be quite clear.
6. Add the desired flavourings and colour.
7. Leave to stand for about 10 minutes. Strain into the tin.
8. Cut into pieces when set and dust liberally with cornflour.
9. After about 3 hours, pack into boxes in icing sugar and sherbert.

Note: This recipe produces a soft Turkish Delight that keeps well.

CREME DE MENTHE (1)

Use recipe for TURKISH DELIGHT (1) but omit the orange and lemon, and add:

5 ml (1 tsp) peppermint essence
or 3–4 drops oil of peppermint

up to 60 ml (4 tbsp) Crème de Menthe
green colouring

CREME DE MENTHE (2)

Use the recipe for TURKISH DELIGHT (2) and add:

up to 150 ml ($^1\!/_4$ pint) Crème de Menthe
green colouring

Note: When using Crème de Menthe, reduce the quantity of water, otherwise the Turkish Delight will not set.

FRUIT JELLIES, JUJUBES & PASTILLES

Fruit jellies are sweetened fruit syrups made from strained or puréed fruit and set with gelatine. **Jujubes** have glucose added to make the confection chewey. **Fruit pastilles** are made from a reduced sweetened purée and are allowed to dry in the air. All are excellent ways of using a glut of fruit, and providing a tasty confection!

Strained fruit gives a clear jelly, whilst puréed fruit produces greater quantity but a cloudy result. The quantity of sugar in fruit jellies and jujubes can be increased or reduced depending on the sharpness of the fruit and personal taste.

Pastilles are similar to fruit cheeses and are sometimes sold in delicatessens as accompaniments to dairy cheese – like eating an apple, or apple pie, with cheese.

Jellies, jujubes and pastilles are set in a wet tin and cut with petits fours cutters or a sharp knife or pair of scissors, and coated with sugar. They keep well in an airtight tin between layers of greaseproof or waxed paper.

ORANGE LIQUEUR JELLIES

900 g (2 lb) granulated sugar
1 pkt gelatine
225 ml (8 fl oz) fresh concentrated orange juice

30 ml (2 tbsp) orange liqueur
30 ml (2 tbsp) water
caster sugar for dusting.

1. Put fruit juice and sugar in a saucepan and dissolve, stirring occasionally until the sugar has dissolved. Bring to the boil (116°C/240°F).
2. Sprinkle gelatine over 30 ml (2 tbsp) water and dissolve over hot water.
3. When dissolved, add gelatine and liqueur to syrup. Pour into an 18 cm (7 ins) square tin which has been rinsed with cold water, and leave to set.
4. Cut into squares and dust with caster sugar.

LIME JELLIES

300 ml ($^1/_2$ pint) undiluted lime cordial   55 g (2 oz) gelatine
225 g (8 oz) granulated sugar   white sugar for coating

1. Place the cordial in a small pan with the sugar and heat slowly until the sugar has dissolved.
2. Sprinkle the gelatine on to 125 ml (4 fl oz) cold water and leave this until it has swollen and softened. Then add the softened gelatine to the lime syrup and stir the mixture on a low heat until the gelatine has dissolved completely.
3. Wet a 20 cm (8 ins) square tin with cold water and pour in the syrup. Leave it in a cool place to set.
4. Turn the jelly on to a surface sprinkled with sugar and cut into shapes and coat with sugar.
5. Store in an airtight container between layers of greaseproof / silicone paper.

   VARIATIONS:
   (a) To flavour, blackcurrant or any other fruit cordial may be used.
   (b) Try apple juice with clove-flavoured sugar (see page 42).
   (c) Replace the sugar with honey, and the cordial with lemon juice.

BLACKCURRANT JUJUBES

450 g (1 lb) blackcurrants   55 g (2 oz) gelatine
150 ml ($^1/_4$ pt) water   60 ml (4 tbsp) water
225 g (8 oz) sugar   caster/granulated sugar for coating
80 ml (3 fl oz) glucose

1. Gently cook the blackcurrants in water for approx. 15 mins.
2. Strain through a fine sieve or jelly bag. This should produce 300 ml ($^1/_2$ pint) juice.
3. Sprinkle the gelatine on to the 60 ml (4 tbsp) water.
4. Heat the juice, sugar and glucose until the sugar has dissolved, and bring to boil.
5. Add the gelatine and stir until thoroughly dissolved.
6. Put the mixture into a wet 20 cm (8 ins) tin.
7. Allow to set.
8. Cut into shapes and coat with sugar.
9. Store in an airtight tin between layers of greaseproof paper.

LEMON / ORANGE JUJUBES

300 ml (½ pint) fresh
    lemon / orange juice (strained)
225 g (8 oz) flavoured sugar
80 ml (3 fl oz) glucose

55 g (2 oz) gelatine
60 ml (4 tbsp) water
caster or granulated sugar for coating

Follow method for BLACKCURRANT JUJUBES (page 41) starting from (3).

Flavoured Sugar – ingredients and method
1. **To 225 g (8 oz) caster or granulated sugar add the thinly peeled zest of 1 grapefruit, or 2 oranges, or 2 lemons, or 4 limes, or 3–4 satsumas.**
2. Store the sugar in an airtight jar. Remove the zest before use.
3. The sugar takes the flavour from the oil in the zest. Use the sugar in cakes, fillings, sweets or any other confections.

APPLE PASTILLES

Cooking apples
Granulated sugar

Icing sugar for dusting

1. Wash the apples. Chop roughly without peeling and coring.
2. Stew the apples in a heavy pan with a little water to prevent burning.
3. When soft, press the fruit through a fine sieve, discarding the peel and pips.
4. Measure purée, place in saucepan, add equal quantity of granulated sugar, cook gently, stirring frequently, until mixture becomes thick and the spoon leaves a trail across the pan base when drawn across it. This may take up to 40 minutes.
5. Pour the mixture into a buttered tin and leave to set.
6. Cut into shapes and toss in sifted icing sugar.

   Flavourings: To be added when the mixture has thickened – cinnamon, ground cloves or grated orange or lemon zest.

FRUIT CHEESE

See page 40, introduction to this section. Follow the recipe and method above, using any fruit, eg. damson, plum, quince. Pour into a greased rectangular loaf tin or container 9 x 18 x 5 cm (3½ x 7½ x 2 ins). Cut into 1 cm (½ inch) slices and serve with dairy cheese.

APRICOT PASTILLES

450 g (1 lb) tinned or fresh apricots
   or 350 g (³/₄ lb) dried apricots
   and 150 ml (¹/₄ pint) apple juice

175 g (6 oz) granulated sugar
10 ml (2 tsp) lemon juice
extra granulated sugar for coating

1. Gently poach fresh or dried apricots in the apple juice until soft, then purée or sieve. Canned fruit should be pressed through a sieve with one-third of the juice from the can.
2. Place purée in a saucepan with sugar and lemon juice. Bring slowly to boil, ensuring all the sugar is dissolved. Continue to boil, stirring frequently until a little of the mixture will set or hold its shape when dropped on to a cold plate.
3. Pour into a wet tin, and leave to set.
4. Turn out of the tin, and cut into suitable shapes.
5. Toss in the sugar to coat.
6. Place in paper cases and store in an airtight container.

QUINCE PASTILLES

Quinces are rich in pectin and are suitable for making pastilles. Ripe quinces are pale yellow, pleasantly perfumed and hard. Quinces are plentiful in some parts of the country, more difficult to get hold of in other parts. If you have difficulty finding quinces, use damsons instead.

680 g (1¹/₂ lb) quinces
150 ml (¹/₄ pint) dry cider or water
450 g (1 lb) granulated sugar
juice of 2 lemons

5 ml (1 tsp) ground cinnamon
2.5 ml (¹/₂ tsp) ground cloves
granulated sugar for dusting

1. Chop the quinces coarsely without peeling or coring, and cook in a pan with the cider or water until the pulp is soft enough to pass easily through a sieve.
2. Strain the purée. Wash the pan and wet a 20 cm (8 ins) square tin.
3. Return the purée to the pan. Add the sugar, lemon juice and spice. Simmer the purée steadily, stirring it often to avoid sticking, until it is very thick. It is ready when a spoon drawn through the mixture leaves a permanent trail.
4. Spread the paste in the wet tin and leave to set for at least 24 hours.
5. Turn on to a surface dusted with granulated sugar. Leave the paste to dry in a warm, airy place at least 24 hours more before cutting into individual sweets.
6. Cut into shapes.
7. Coat pastilles in sugar and leave until quite dry before packing them.

CHOCOLATES

What better way to enhance your sweet-making achievements than by turning them into delectable, mouth-watering chocolates – the classic finish! Today, the enthusiastic amateur can now accomplish in her own kitchen, without needing specialised equipment or ingredients, what has previously been regarded as only possible in the professional conditions of the modern factory.

Before beginning, and in order to achieve the best possible results, it is essential to understand how chocolate is made and the characteristics of the various types available.

Chocolate consists of two main ingredients, both extracted from cocoa beans – the seeds of the large pods produced by the cacao tree. After the pods are harvested, the beans are removed, fermented and roasted, then pressed to extract the cocoa powder and a brittle white fat known as cocoa butter. These are then re-amalgamated in varying proportions, with the addition of sweeteners, dairy or other fats, and some milk solids, to produce the various types of chocolate available to us.

The finest quality and most superior flavoured chocolate, used by professionals, is known as **Couverture** and contains a high proportion of cocoa solids. In order to ensure Couverture chocolates set well with a high gloss, it must go through a process known as 'tempering'.

The percentage of cocoa solids in Couverture chocolate is as follows:

Extra dark bitter   *70%*
Dark sweet bitter   *60%*
Light   *38%*

The higher the percentage of cocoa solids, the lower the percentage of fat. Many branded makes state the percentage of cocoa solids present and the percentage and type of fat in the product.

ALTERNATIVE CHOCOLATES FOR COATING

For the home chocolate maker, a very acceptable alternative is available, known by a variety of names such as **Compound chocolate**, **Dipping or Confectioner's chocolate**, or simply **Chocolate flavoured covering**. This contains less cocoa butter than Couverture chocolate but has added vegetable or dairy fats and does not require the tempering process to produce an acceptable, well-flavoured, glossy result.

CHOCOLATE FLAVOURED BARS, frequently found on supermarket shelves, contain even more added vegetable fats. These produce a much softer chocolate, suitable for using as a cooking ingredient or for a cake coating, since its softer texture prevents its shattering when cut into. However, the added fats impair the flavour. It will not set crisp, which makes it disappointing as a coating for centres.

DESSERT CHOCOLATE, made for eating (the commercial bars), contains a good amount of cocoa butter for flavour but remains too thick for coating centres when melted, and usually sets with a duller surface. It can, however, be piped more easily than dipping chocolate and therefore can be used more successfully for decoration.

MILK CHOCOLATE for dipping is also available and is made by the addition of milk solids, butter fat and sugar. It can remain rather thick when melted but this can usually be overcome by the addition of a very small quantity of white fat.

WHITE CHOCOLATE is a mixture of cocoa butter, milk and sugar, and behaves in a similar way to milk chocolate.

CAROB CHOCOLATE (caffeine free) is also available, usually from health food outlets. It does not need tempering but does not produce a glossy appearance when set.

Notes about Suppliers:
(a) Couverture is not readily available but can be obtained from certain specialist outlets. (eg. Terence Fisher, Unit 23, Earl Soham Business Park, Suffolk IP13 7SA. Tel. 01728 685955)
(b) Dipping chocolate is easily obtained from Sugarcraft suppliers and can be found in various forms – there are solid blocks which should be finely broken up or grated before melting, or more often there are 'buttons' or small drops.

TEMPERING COUVERTURE CHOCOLATE

The process used for tempering chocolate below, although relatively simple, should be followed correctly. The instructions for tempering Couverture chocolate are normally included with the chocolate.

1. Using a 300 g (10½ oz) bar of Couverture chocolate, grate 80 g (3 oz) into a dry bowl, and chop the rest of the chocolate finely.
2. Put the chopped chocolate into a bowl and heat it slowly over a pan of warm water (not hot) to 38°C/100°F, stirring all the time. Do not allow any water or steam to fall on the chocolate as it is being worked – damp atmosphere coats the chocolate with a 'bloom'. The bottom of the bowl in which you are heating the chocolate should feel just warm, and you have better control over the heat in the bowl if it does not touch the water.
3. Remove the bowl from the heat before all the lumps of chocolate have melted. To avoid water droplets getting near the chocolate, dry the bottom of the bowl when you remove it from the heat. Check the temperature of the chocolate with a thermometer (38°C/100°F). If it has not reached this temperature, heat again.
4. While the bowl is off the heat, add the grated chocolate, give it a good stir, then return it over the saucepan of hot water to bring heat back to 31°C/88°F, stirring all the time until it becomes smooth.
5. Leave for 5 minutes off the heat, give it a good stir, then re-heat to 31°C/88°F.
6. This is now ready to use in moulds.

HINTS FOR SUCCESSFUL CHOCOLATE DIPPING

Chocolate and moisture are deadly enemies, so choose a time and place in which to do the dipping of your centres when no moisture is apparent – a steam-free kitchen on a fine but not over-warm day.

The prepared centres should not be cold nor should their surfaces be damp. To be certain of this, they should have been made at least a day earlier and allowed to stand in airy conditions in order to form a slightly thin crust. There should be no stickiness felt when they are handled.

Fudges and fondants will dry naturally; others, such as marzipan, can be given a light dusting with cornflour to assist the drying process.

1. **Melting process:**
   (a) Set a saucepan containing about 5 cm (2 ins) of water to boil. When boiling, remove from the heat.
   (b) Place the bowl, containing the prepared chocolate (225 g / 8 oz) on the pan. It should fit snugly, to avoid steam escaping, but must not touch the water. When melted, the chocolate should be approx. 49°C/120°F when tested with a thermometer.
   (c) Remove the bowl from the pan. You should be able to hold the bowl in your cupped hands without flinching, and feel moderate warmth. The chocolate should remain sufficiently liquid for dipping 30–40 centres, but the bowl may be returned to the pan for a short time should the chocolate begin to set round the edges.
   (d) While the dipping process is carried out, the chocolate should be frequently stirred to prevent the separation of the fats and cocoa solids within it which cause streaks to appear.

2. **Dipping:**
   (a) Place the centres on a greaseproof or foil-lined tray, to one side of the bowl of chocolate, and a foil-lined tray to receive the chocolates on the other side.
   (b) Starting with the centres which are least likely to shed crumbs, such as Brazils and fondants, drop one at a time into the chocolate, ensuring that each is totally immersed, then lift out with a fork.
   (c) Tap the fork gently on the side of the bowl, easing the centre towards the tip and shaking off the excess chocolate. Draw the fork across the rim of the bowl to remove the last drips.
   (d) Alternatively, wipe the underside of the fork with a skewer. This prevents the chocolate being distributed all round the edge of the bowl, which makes it very messy.
   (e) Allow the coated centre to slide from the fork on to the second foil-lined tray, giving it a very slight push forward if necessary to cover a possible drip. Leave to set. Always place the first centres furthest away and work towards you to avoid disasters if later chocolates happen to fall.

3. **Appropriate decorations:**
   (a) Decorations such as a flaked almond or a sliver of crystallized fruit, can be added before the chocolate sets.
   (b) Other centres may be marked with the fork after dipping to give them identity. The side of the fork can be laid across the surface of the centre and then lifted before it sets, leaving a raised line. If the fork is moved slightly sideways as it is lifted, the line will have a raised peak. Several parallel lines can be achieved by using the underside of the fork.

(c) Special dipping forks can be obtained, which can achieve a variety of patterns. These are, in effect, simply twisted lengths of wire inserted into a wooden dowelling handle and could easily be made by an amateur craftsman.

(d) A contrasting chocolate (eg. milk or plain) can be melted, placed in a piping bag, then drizzled over the chocolate's surface, but this must be done quickly before it has time to set.

4. **The final stage:**

(a) The coated centres must be left until quite firm before they are removed from the foil-lined tray.

(b) They should never be lifted with the fingers unless gloves are worn, or they will be marked. Always lift them with a flat-bladed knife and place them directly into the brown glacine paper cases which can be obtained from Sugarcraft suppliers and are sold specifically for this purpose.

CENTRES SUITABLE FOR COATING

TYPE OF CHOCOLATE AND DECORATION:

Centre	see page	Chocolate for Coating	Decoration
Peppermint cream	18	plain, whole or half dipped	use dipping fork
Coffee fondants	17	plain	piped milk chocolate or half almond
Orange fondants	15–16	plain	candied orange peel
Lemon creams	15–16	plain	crystallized lemon
Rosehip creams	15–16	plain	crystallized rose petal
Marzipan balls	58	plain	slither of roasted almond
Marzipan walnuts	61	plain	walnut half
Vanilla fudge	19	plain	walnut or almond
Nut/fruit fudge	20	milk	piped plain chocolate
Date fudge (nut/fruit)	20	plain	dipping fork
Ginger fudge (nut/fruit)	20	plain	crystallized ginger
Cream caramels	28,29	milk	piped plain chocolate
Soft vanilla creams	16	plain	almond half
Truffles	53–56,74	milk or plain	leave plain

LIQUEUR CHOCOLATES

Chocolate liqueurs are a real luxury and need not be difficult to produce. They are made by forming a shell of chocolate into which a small quantity of spirit, liqueur or liqueur syrup is poured; it is then sealed in with a layer of chocolate.

300 g (10^1/$_2$ oz) plain tempered chocolate
450 g (1 lb) granulated sugar
30 ml (2 tbsp) approx. liqueur per preserving jar (see below)
    of your own choice, eg. Rum, Kirsch, Cherry Brandy, Grand Marnier

For the sugar syrup:
1. Dissolve 450 g (1 lb) granulated sugar in 120 ml (8 tbsp) of water in a small pan over heat. Do not let it boil until all the sugar has dissolved. Have ready a pan of water and brush, as the sugar liquid starts to boil, and wash the inside of the pan with the wet brush to remove the crystals. The sugar liquid should reach 108°C/225°F to form syrup. Check on thermometer.
2. If different flavours are required, pour equally into warm screw-top jars, add liqueur and seal jars. Mix the liqueur with the syrup by turning the sealed jar gently.
3. Cool by just leaving for a few hours or by placing at first in tepid water and then in cold water.
4. It is advisable to make the syrup in small quantities, as sugar crystals will re-form if the syrup is stored for any length of time. If the syrup does crystallize, use to cook fruit.

TO FILL THE MOULDS

1. You will need suitable moulds, which can be obtained from Sugarcraft shops. These are usually made of plastic, in the form of a small tray containing about 9 bottle- or barrel-shaped indentations. These moulds need no preparation other than a polish with a clean, dry tissue, since the polishing gives a gloss to the chocolate surface.

2. The moulds are filled with melted chocolate. As the outer edges begin to solidify the remaining liquid chocolate is drained back into the bowl by inverting the moulds, which are then laid flat, still inverted, on kitchen foil. This causes any remaining liquid chocolate to run down to form a small lip around the edge of the bottle or barrel shape, and aids the sealing process later.

3. The following advice may appear somewhat drastic but I find the process of filling the moulds, described above, is made much easier if, before use, the tray of moulds is cut up into individual shapes, which then have to be balanced on cups or glasses, or cut up into pairs of shapes, which helps to make them more stable. This is done because, by the time the last indentation in the tray is being filled, the first will be starting to harden, so all of them will not be able to drain at the same time.

4. Leave the shells in a cool place to harden – a few minutes in the refrigerator should achieve this.

5. Remove the foil and gently trickle into the moulds the desired liqueur or spirit, to about $3/4$ full.

6. Take a small piece of kitchen foil and spread with a patch of melted chocolate approx. 3 mm ($1/8$ inch) deep and sufficient to cover the individual mould. Press the inverted, chocolate-covered foil down on to the filled mould and run your finger round the edges of the mould to ensure a good seal. Since the moulds are transparent, it is possible to peep underneath to check the seal is satisfactory.

7. Put the moulds back in the refrigerator to finish setting.

8. As the chocolate hardens, it shrinks slightly, and so the liqueurs can be released with a gentle tap. Any excess chocolate will probably break away but the edge can be smoothed off very carefully with the fingers. Avoid touching the upper surface of the liqueurs, as this will spoil the gloss. Handle them, if necessary, with a soft tissue. If any leaks or cracks are apparent, they can be patched with a little melted chocolate.

9. Liqueurs can be presented on an attractive dish for immediate consumption. For packing, they can be individually wrapped in coloured foil, if you can find a supply, which makes them look particularly luxurious.

10. The foil used for wrapping sweets and chocolates is thinner and more pliable than kitchen foil. To identify the liqueurs used in the chocolates, cover each liqueur type of chocolate with different coloured foil. Add an important and really professional touch by designing a chart of the different types and including this in your box of liqueur chocolates.

LIQUEUR SYRUP

If you prefer to fill the liqueurs with a liqueur syrup, it should be prepared as follows:

110 g (4 oz) granulated sugar
30 ml (2 tbsp) cold water
15 ml (1 tbsp) liqueur

1. Have ready a small warmed jar which has a good sealing lid –a 350 g (12 oz) jam jar is ideal – and a supply of ice cubes.
2. Following the rules for sugar boiling (pages 9–11), place the sugar and water in a small pan, then boil the syrup to 108°C/225°F. Remove from the heat and pour into the warmed jar.
3. Add the liqueur and immediately seal the jar. Turn the jar gently a few times to fully mix in the liqueur. Do not shake the jar, as this will encourage the syrup to crystallize.
4. Place the sealed jar in a bowl containing lukewarm water. Gradually add the ice cubes to aid the rapid cooling of the syrup. When cold, the syrup is ready to use.

Notes:
(a) In some recipes, you will find that after the shells are filled with syrup they are left for about 24 hours for the syrup to form a sugary crust, so that melted chocolate can be spread on it. I find this time-consuming and unnecessary, and prefer the simpler method above. Moreover, once the crystallizing process begins in the syrup it is possible for it to continue once the chocolate is sealed – how disappointing to find, when biting into a chocolate liqueur, that it contains nothing but sugar crystals!

(b) Some recipes also recommend coating the moulds with chocolate by brushing them with melted chocolate, using a small artist's brush. Experience has persuaded me that this is not easy, as the chocolate sets very quickly on the paint brush, clogging it up and rendering it difficult to use without frequent cleaning. There is also the danger of the brush hairs becoming dislodged and reappearing in finished chocolate – not to be recommended!

FRUITY CHOCOLATES

80 g (3 oz) plain chocolate　　　　　**25 g (1 oz) finely chopped cherries**
25 g (1 oz) chopped ginger　　　　　**15 ml (1 tbsp) brandy or liqueur of choice**

1. Melt 40 g (1½ oz) chocolate. Drop 12–14 small chocolate rounds on to greaseproof paper and flatten, or drop chocolate into petits fours cases. Leave to set.
2. Mix the fruit with the brandy. Form the fruit mixture into balls and press to the same diameter as the chocolate rounds. Place on top of the chocolate rounds.
3. Melt the remaining chocolate, and then spoon into a piping bag fitted with a fine nozzle, and pipe a lattice over each chocolate, or drop the chocolate from a spoon.
4. Decorate with ginger or cherry. Leave to set.
5. Store layered with greaseproof paper for up to three weeks in an airtight container.

COLLETTES

Collettes can be made in petits fours cases or in queen cake cases.

1. Take two cases, one inside the other and, using a pastry brush, brush the inside with melted chocolate.
2. Turn the cases upside down on paper until the chocolate has set.
3. Coat as many of the cases as required. Surplus cases will keep well in an airtight tin.
4. When set, brush again with a second layer of chocolate and turn upside down.
5. When set again, remove the paper cases carefully.
6. Fill with desired filling.

> **Note:** Petits fours cases may be used, for example, in:
> p.40　Jellies, etc.
> p.54　Truffles
> p.58　Marzipan
> p.72　Ganache

See also Chocolate Raisin Cups and Coconut & Cherry Petits Fours, p.69.

TRUFFLES

Classic truffles consist of a chocolate paste called **ganache**, which is made by combining melted chocolate and warmed cream, and adding flavours. The firmness of the paste is achieved by the correct proportion of cream to chocolate, and by the types of chocolate and cream used.

225 g (8 oz) dark chocolate with 150 ml (¼ pint) of double cream will produce a reasonably firm paste. If whipping cream, or an equal mixture of single and double cream, is used, this must be reduced to 80 ml (3 fl oz). Similarly, if milk chocolate is used, 225 g (8 oz) will accept not more than 175 ml (6 fl oz) of whipping cream.

When the truffles are formed, they are given a thin coating of cocoa powder to make them easy to handle, then they are dipped in chocolate and/or given a further coating such as ground nuts, coconut, icing sugar, grated chocolate, chocolate vermicelli, etc.

Classic truffles do not keep above a week or two, so they should be stored in a refrigerator, but the flavour tends to diminish when they are chilled. They can be frozen but care must be taken in thawing. This must be done very slowly to prevent condensation forming.

The recipe for CLASSIC TRUFFLES is given first. The other recipes in this section, though not classic truffles themselves, will make excellent basic pastes which can be formed into truffles. They all keep very well in the refrigerator and can be used when desired. They also freeze very well.

CLASSIC TRUFFLES

225 g (8 oz) milk chocolate
80 ml (3 fl oz) whipping cream
    or **20 ml (4 tsp) single cream**
    and 60 ml (4 tbsp) double cream, combined
60 ml (4 tbsp) cocoa, sieved together with 15 ml (1 tbsp) icing sugar.

1. Heat some water in a pan until it reaches 72°C/160°F, with large bubbles just appearing.
2. Remove from the heat and place in a bowl containing the chocolate over the pan. The water must not touch the bowl. Stir the chocolate until it has melted.
3. Meanwhile, in another pan, bring the cream to the boil, then cool to 44°C/110°F, and stir into the melted chocolate. Allow the mixture to cool to 30°C/65°F, stirring occasionally. Beat with an electric mixer until the paste becomes fluffy and the colour has lightened. Refrigerate for 5–10 minutes until it is firm enough to shape by hand.
4. Coat a tray with a generous layer of sweetened cocoa. Using 2 teaspooons, drop lumps of the paste on to the cocoa-covered tray. Lightly roll the lumps of paste into balls with your fingertips. Coat with a second coating of chopped nuts, grated chocolate, coconut, etc., and place in paper cases.
5. If it is intended to dip the truffles in melted chocolate, they should not be given the second coating but should be left in a cool place for a day or so until a light crust has formed on them. They can be dipped in melted chocolate (see CHOCOLATE section, page 49).

FRUIT & NUT TRUFFLES

80 g (3 oz) blanched almonds
175 g (6 oz) dried mixed fruit
5 ml (1 tsp) sherry, brandy or rum
approx. 80 g (3 oz) toasted desiccated coconut

1. Chop the nuts finely. Mince or finely chop the fruit and mix with the nuts.
2. Add the sherry and bind the mixture together.
3. Divide the mixture into about 12 portions and mould firmly into even-sized balls.
4. Roll in toasted coconut and leave to set.

ORANGE LIQUEUR TRUFFLES

55 g (2 oz) chocolate
55 g (2 oz) unsalted butter
140 g (5 oz) orange flavour icing sugar

5 ml (1 tsp) Grand Marnier or Cointreau
grated white chocolate for coating

1. Melt the chocolate and butter over a low heat
2. Add the icing sugar and flavouring
3. Allow to set. Shape and coat.

RUM TRUFFLES (1)

55 g (2 oz) plain chocolate
55 g (2 oz) ground almonds
2.5 ml ($^{1}/_{2}$ tsp) liquid glucose
22.5 ml ($1^{1}/_{2}$ tbsp) caster sugar
2.5 ml ($^{1}/_{2}$ tsp) cream

flavourings – rum (or brandy, sherry, coffee, etc.
coatings – chocolate vermicelli, chocolate powder, etc.

1. Melt the chocolate in a basin over hot water.
2. Add the remaining ingredients and mix well.
3. Roll into balls and toss in coating mixture.

   ALTERNATIVE COATING:
   (a) Roll the balls a little smaller than above. Leave to dry overnight, then dip in melted chocolate and toss in chocolate vermicelli.
   (b) This method produces about 24 truffles.

RUM TRUFFLES (2)

55 g (2 oz) plain chocolate
55 g (2 oz) icing sugar
25 g (1 oz) sponge crumbs
25 g (1 oz) cocoa powder

55 g (2 oz) unsalted butter
5 ml (1 tsp) instant coffee
5 ml (1 tsp) rum

1. Melt the chocolate and butter over hot water. Stir gently.
2. Add 55 g (2 oz) sugar, coffee, rum and crumbs until required consistency.
3. Chill for 30 minutes.
4. Roll into even-sized balls and place on a baking sheet. Return to fridge.
5. Coat thickly in cocoa powder or icing sugar. Place in cases.

RICH RUM TRUFFLES

225 g (8 oz) plain chocolate   10 ml (2 tsp) single cream
25 g (1 oz) unsalted butter   10 ml (2 tsp) rum
2 egg yolks

1. Melt chocolate in a bowl over hot water. Add rest of ingredients. Mix together.
2. Allow the water to simmer for 5 mins to cook the egg yolk.
3. Leave to cool and thicken, enough to handle.
4. Form into balls and roll in vermicelli. Place in sweet cases.

VARIATIONS:
(a) Replace rum with sherry, whisky, brandy or liqueurs.
(b) Replace vermicelli with chocolate powder, chopped nuts, coconut toasted or coloured, dipped in royal icing or melted chocolate.
(c) Replace milk and alcohol with 10 ml (2 tsp) orange juice and grated rind of an orange.
(d) Fruit that has been soaked in liqueurs may be added to the truffles.
(e) Add 25 g (1 oz) chopped crystallized ginger

CAROB TRUFFLES
(makes about 10)

45 ml (3 tbsp) unsweetened carob powder
30 ml (2 tbsp) clear honey
25 g (1 oz) skimmed milk powder
30 ml (2 tbsp) single cream
55 g (2 oz) desiccated coconut

Coating: carob powder with ground cinnamon

1. Blend the carob powder, honey and skimmed milk in a bowl over hot water.
2. Remove from heat. Beat in the cream.
3. Gradually work in the icing sugar and coconut.
4. Cover and chill until firm enough to handle.
5. Form into balls, coat and chill.

Note: Carob is a flour made from the carob pod. It is a good source of carbohydrate and calcium and contains no stimulants. Carob bars are made from carob flour and coconut oil.

MARZIPAN

Marzipan is a delectable paste for making sweets and when presented as a selection of modelled, miniature fruits it can be temptingly attractive. Uncooked marzipan (almond paste) is not as easy to shape as cooked marzipan, which can be moulded and rolled out into a variety of shapes that can be coated with chocolate.

Home-made, cooked marzipan is preferable for sweet-making, since the ready-made kind obtainable from supermarkets, while it is excellent for many other purposes (eg. cake covering), tends to be heavily flavoured with almond, making the introduction of other flavours, in order to produce a variety of sweets or chocolate centres, somewhat ineffectual. Marzipan fruits made by commercial suppliers are rarely appropriately flavoured – they all taste alike – but the home-made ones can be given flavours in keeping with their kind.

Colouring of fruits is usually done by painting with vegetable colourings, using a clean, soft artist's brush. Colour and flavour are introduced to sweets at the same time, working these into the paste together. Marzipan fruits are usually packaged on their own, not in an assortment of sweets, as the applied colour may transfer.

Shaped marzipan sweets are not often found in mixed assortments unless they have been crystallized, as they rapidly dry out when exposed to air. They keep moist and soft longer if coated with chocolate.

See also CENTRES SUITABLE FOR COATING *(page 48)*

MARZIPAN

This recipe will produce about 450 g (1 lb) of marzipan, which will make about 70 centres for chocolate dripping.

225 g (8 oz) granulated sugar   **1 egg white**
5 ml (1 tsp) liquid glucose   **100 ml (4 fl oz) water**
175 g (6 oz) ground almonds

1. Follow the rules for sugar boiling (pages 9–11), thoroughly dissolve the sugar in the water, add the glucose and boil the syrup to 116°C/240°F soft ball stage. Remove from the heat and check the boil.
2. Stir in the ground almonds – all at once. Then stir in the UNBEATEN egg white. Return to a low heat and cook for 2–4 minutes, stirring to prevent burning. The longer cooking time should be employed if the mixture looks very slack. It should have the appearance of very thick porridge.
3. Turn the mixture out on to a dish or slab or work surface and turn with a spatula (as for fondant) until the paste thickens and is cool and firm enough to be moulded by the fingers without feeling sticky. Knead to a smooth paste, dusting with sifted icing sugar to control any stickiness.
4. If you have the use of a food mixer, the working and kneading can be done very successfully in it, using the normal beater or the dough hook. This cuts down considerably on time and energy.
5. Wrap the marzipan in wax paper or clingfilm and store in an airtight container in a cool place. It will keep for months in a refrigerator and can be very successfully frozen.
6. The paste can now be divided up, the portions coloured and flavoured as desired, and rolled or moulded into numerous shapes.

MARZIPAN CENTRES FOR CHOCOLATES

The following are just a few suggestions for creating centres for chocolates.

ALMOND TUBS
No colour. Flavour with a few drops of ratafia. Roll out to 5 mm (¼ inch) thick and cut into small rounds:

BANANA CRESCENTS
Colour yellow, flavour with banana essence and cut into crescent shapes.

COFFEE CUSHIONS

Flavour and colour with coffee essence or strong dissolved instant coffee. Beware of making the mixture too wet. If the colour looks very pale, it can be darkened with a drop or two of liquid gravy browning. Roll into a long sausage shape, about 2 cm ($^3/_4$ inch) think, then cut it at angles all along the length to form triangles.

PISTACHIO TWISTS

Colour green and flavour with pistachio essence. Form into two thin ropes about 1 cm ($^1/_2$ inch) thick. Twist these together and cut into sections 3 cm ($1^1/_4$ inch) long.

ORANGES

Colour orange and flavour with orange or tangerine essence. A little very finely grated orange zest will improve the flavour. Form into balls and roll them on a nutmeg grater to give the authentic 'orange peel' finish. Remove a clove head and insert in the 'orange'.

Note: Left-over scraps can be combined to make interesting blends of colour and flavour.

DECORATIONS

When the prepared centres are dry, they can be dipped in chocolate and can be decorated as appropriate before the chocolate coating sets.

Almond Tubs: a piece of flaked almond.
Coffee Cushions: a small piece of walnut.
Pistachio Twists: sprinkle with chopped pistachio nuts; alternatively dip only one end of the twist in the chocolate.
Oranges: dip these in melted chocolate only up to their waists.

MARZIPAN FRUITS

When making marzipan fruits, colour $^1/_4$ mixture green; for pears and apples, colour remainder yellow. Keep $^1/_4$ for bananas. Add a few drops cochineal and blend thoroughly. Keep $^1/_2$ for golden apples, apricots and peaches. Use $^1/_2$ for tangerines – add more cochineal for tangerines and oranges.

Apples: Colour green or paint with food colour after shaping. Use 2 cloves, one for the stalk end and one for the other end.

Pears: Colour green. Shape end point. Use clove.

Apricots: Shape, using the blunt end of a knife to mark the groove.

Peaches: As above. Paint to give rosy shading. Sprinkle with icing sugar.

Bananas: Colour yellow. Shape individually and form into a bunch. Paint tips and edges with thick coffee to give ripe appearance.

Note: All fruits should be a similar size.

BOILED MARZIPAN

Makes 900 g (2 lb)

450 g (1 lb) granulated sugar
350 g (12 oz) ground almonds
80 g (3 oz) sieved icing sugar

150 ml ($^1/_4$ pint) water
2 egg whites, NOT beaten
pinch of cream of tartar

1. Dissolve the sugar in the water in a heavy-based saucepan. Bring to the boil and add cream of tartar and boil to 116°C/240°F soft ball stage.
2. Remove the pan from the heat and stir in ground almonds and egg whites, returning to the heat to cook for a few more minutes, stirring well.
3. Turn on to a flat surface dusted with sieved icing sugar, lifting the edges of the mixture if sufficiently cool. Knead until cool.
4. This will keep wrapped in greaseproof paper. Ideal for modelling flowers and animals.

CHOCOLATE MARZIPAN FRUITS AND NUTS

home-made or bought marzipan
selection of assorted nuts and glacé fruits
chocolate for dipping

1. Take small quantities of marzipan and surround the fruit or nut. Shape. Leave for a few minutes to 'set'.
2. Melt a small quantity of chocolate in a bowl over hot water. Stir until smooth and free running.
3. Dip marzipan-covered fruits. Allow excess chocolate to roll off.
4. Place on greaseproof paper to harden.

NUTTY CHERRY ROLLS

225 g (8 oz) marzipan
55 g (2 oz) glacé cherries
55 g (2 oz) melted chocolate
55 g (2 oz) blanched almonds,
    chopped and toasted

15 g ($^{1}/_{2}$ oz) cocoa powder
green colouring

1. Divide marzipan into three parts. Colour one piece green, leave the second plain, and blend the cocoa into the third.
2. Roll out each piece to about 3 mm ($^{1}/_{8}$ inch) thick and 6 cm ($2^{1}/_{2}$ ins) wide. Layer them – white, green and brown on top.
3. Place a line of cherries (washed and dried) along the length. Roll up from the long edge as if making a Swiss roll. Brush with the melted chocolate, then roll in the toasted almonds. Put in a cool place to harden. Cut into 1 cm ($^{1}/_{2}$ inch) slices. This can be made a week in advance and left wrapped and uncut.

VARIATIONS:
Flavour with coffee, fill with glacé pineapple, coat with coconut. Nutty roll can be made even more luxurious by brushing the layers of marzipan with apricot jam or sherry.

MARZIPAN WALNUTS

55 g (2 oz) marzipan
55 g (2 oz) walnuts

1. Colour the marzipan with green, pink or orange colouring to give a pastel shade.
2. Break off small pieces of the marzipan and roll each piece into a ball. Flatten slightly.
3. Place a half walnut on either side of the marzipan and press the two sides together.
4. Place in a sweet case and leave to one side.

MARZIPAN DATES

Remove the stone from dessert dates and fill with a piece of marzipan.

COCONUT ICE

Coconut ice is easy to make but tends to be very sweet. Avoid overcooking, otherwise it becomes dry and crumbly. The cooked version keeps well and is suitable for coating with chocolate.

350 g (12 oz) granulated sugar **110 g (4 oz) dessicated coconut**
150 ml (¼ pint) water **15 ml (1 tbsp) liquid glucose**
pink colouring

1. Dissolve sugar in water, add glucose, boil to 115°C/238°F.
2. Stir in all the coconut at once. Pour into an 18 cm (7 ins) greased square tin.
3. Make a second quantity, add pink colouring with the coconut and pour over the white.
4. Leave to set and cut out when cold.

VARIATIONS:

CHERRY COCONUT ICE
Add 110 g (4 oz) glacé cherries just before the mixture reaches 115°C/238°F.

HARLEQUIN COCONUT ICE
Add 55 g (2 oz) chopped glacé cherries and 55 g (2 oz) chopped angelica just before the mixture reaches 115°C/238°F.

CHOCOLATE COCONUT ICE
Add 55–80 g (2–3 oz) chocolate powder just before the mixture reaches 115°C/238°F. Stir well until absorbed, then add the coconut.

COFFEE COCONUT ICE
Use 150 ml (¼ pint) strong coffee instead of 150 ml (¼ pint) water.

TOASTED COCONUT CARAMELS

450 g (1 lb) caster sugar
150 ml (¼ pint) water

pinch cream of tartar
55–110 g (2–4 oz) dessicated coconut

1. Put sugar, water and cream of tartar into a heavy-based pan. Stir over a low heat until the sugar has dissolved, and boil to 118°C/244°F firm ball stage.
2. Stir in the coconut and continue stirring until the mixture becomes cloudy.
3. Pour into a well-oiled tin, 20 cm (8 ins) square.
4. When cool, cut into squares. Leave until cold and firm. Put tin under a hot grill for a few seconds. Then turn on to a baking tray and toast on all sides.
5. Cool. Store in a tin.

COCONUT BARS

80 g (3 oz) cream cheese
55g (2 oz) raw brown sugar

110 g (4 oz) desiccated coconut
55 g (2 oz) mixed nuts, finely ground

1. Mix the ingredients together evenly
2. Shape into a bar. Cut into about 20 pieces. Lay on greaseproof paper to dry.

Note: This wholefood coconut ice will keep in the refrigerator for about a week.

UNCOOKED COCONUT ICE

110 g (4 oz) condensed milk
350 g (12 oz) icing sugar

175 g (6 oz) dessicated coconut
cochineal or green colouring

1. Mix condensed milk and icing sugar. Stir in coconut and divide the mixture.
2. Colour one half of the mixture pink or green.
3. Shape the mixture into two identical bars and press firmly together.
4. Place coconut ice on a tray which is covered with silicone paper until firm.
5. Cut as required. Store in refrigerator.

COOKED COCONUT ICE

Omit the sugar (above), double the quantity of condensed milk and coconut, and bake at 190°C/375°F/Gas 5 for 10–15 minutes until golden brown.

MISCELLANEOUS

CHERRY CUPS

18 glacé cherries soaked in sherry or brandy
110 g (4 oz) chocolate for coating

1. Halve 6 cherries and chop others into small pieces.
2. Place sweet cases in twos. Coat inside with melted chocolate. Allow to set.
3. Place chopped cherries into the cases and top up with melted chocolate.
4. Place half a cherry on top and leave to set.

CHOCOLATE ORANGE STICKS

zest of 1 orange   **110 g (4 oz) plain chocolate**
110–150 g (4–5 oz) chocolate

1. Wash and dry the orange.
2. Peel zest of orange and cut into strips $2\frac{1}{2}$ cm (1 inch) long x 2.5 mm ($\frac{1}{10}$ inch).
3. Cover with water and cook until tender.
4. Drain and measure 60 ml (4 tbsp) liquid. Add the sugar, stir until dissolved and boil for 2 mins.
5. Add the cooked orange strips and simmer until all the syrup is absorbed.
6. Dry the strips on a piece of silicone paper in a warm atmosphere.
7. Melt the chocolate and coat the strips.
8. Allow to set on silicone paper. Ensure the strips are straight on the paper.

   Note: A good way to use orange zest; this has a flavoursome, crunchy centre.

BITTER ALMOND CLUSTERS

55 g (2 oz) almonds, sliced   **25 g (1 oz) crystallized ginger**
80 g (3 oz) plain chocolate

1. Toast blanched almonds until golden, cool and cut lengthways into slivers.
2. Melt plain chocolate, stir in almonds and finely chopped ginger.
3. Mix well, then make 12 rough mounds of the mixture on greaseproof paper.
4. Leave to set and then put in sweet cases.

CHOCOLATE CHERRIES

125 g (4¹/₂ oz) jar of Maraschino cherries
110 g (4 oz) plain chocolate
15 g (¹/₂ oz) chopped pistachio nuts

1. Drain cherries and lay on greaseproof paper or kitchen foil.
2. Drop cherries into melted chocolate and coat.
3. While still wet, sprinkle with nuts.

CHOCOLATE WALNUTS

55 g (2 oz) butter
110 g (4 oz) icing sugar
55 g (2 oz) chopped walnuts
80 g (3 oz) coconut

2.5 ml (¹/₂ tsp) instant coffee granules
dissolved in a few drops boiling water
150 g (5 oz) melted chocolate

1. Cream butter and sugar and add dissolved coffee granules, walnuts and coconut.
2. Roll to 1 cm (¹/₂ inch) thickness. Cut into squares.
3. When set, dip in melted chocolate and decorate with pieces of walnut.

CHOCOLATE MINT CRISPS

55 g (2 oz) granulated sugar
2–3 drops oil of peppermint
50 ml (2 fl oz) water

225 g (8 oz) plain chocolate
75 ml (2¹/₂ fl oz) double cream
drinking chocolate powder to dust

1. Line a 15 cm (6 ins) square tin with parchment.
2. Put sugar and water in a small, heavy pan. Heat gently until sugar dissolves.
3. Boil without stirring until golden brown.
4. Cool pan and add 2–3 drops oil of peppermint.
5. Pour on to baking sheet. When hard, place between greaseproof paper and crush with a rolling pin.
6. Melt the chocolate.
7. Put cream in a small pan and bring to the boil.
8. Pour cream on to melted chocolate. Beat until well mixed.
9. Add crushed peppermint mixture and beat for 2 minutes.
10. Turn into a prepared tin. Smooth the surface. Leave overnight.
11. Cut into squares with a sharp knife.

CRYSTALLIZED FLOWERS
(makes plenty, say 50 rose petals)

5 ml (1 tsp) gum arabic
10 ml (2 tsp) rosewater
225 g (8 oz) caster sugar
fresh, dry flowers in perfect condition

1. Put the gum arabic and rosewater into a very small dish and stir until the resin has dissolved completely.
2. Spread some of the caster sugar on a plate and put some of the remainder in a small sieve or coffee strainer.
3. If candying roses or other fairly large flowers, separate into petals and nip off the white heel at base of each petal. Very small flowers, individual lilac flowers, lobelia, violets and primroses can be crystallized whole.
4. Store in airtight container between layers of greaseproof paper. Use for decorating chocolate coated sweets (page 48), cakes and other confections.

CHOCOLATE PRALINE

80 g (3 oz) unblanched almonds   **200 g (7 oz) plain chocolate**
80 g (3 oz) caster sugar   **200 g (7 oz) cooking chocolate**

1. Oil a baking sheet.
2. Gently heat together in a pan the almonds and sugar. Stir to prevent the sugar from sticking. Continue to heat until the sugar caramelises to a golden colour. The nuts should be lightly toasted.
3. Pour on to the baking sheet and leave to set.
4. When hard, crush with a rolling pin.
5. Melt the plain chocolate.
6. Mix in the praline to make a stiff paste.
7. Turn into 18 cm (7 ins) square tin. Leave to set.
8. Cut into squares.
9. Melt the cooking chocolate.
10. Dip the praline, and decorate with slice of toasted almond.

Note: May be left plain and stored layered between greaseproof paper in an airtight container. May also be crushed and incorporated in ice cream or fillings for cakes or other confections.

MIMOSA CHOCOLATE ROSETTES

80 g (3 oz) butter
110 g (4 oz) icing sugar
150 g (5 oz) plain chocolate

175 g (6 oz) cake crumbs
mimosa balls

1. Cream butter and icing sugar together.
2. Melt the chocolate over a pan of hot water in a bowl, or in the microwave, then stir into the butter cream and gradually add cake crumbs.
3. Spoon mixture into piping bag and pipe rosettes into sweet cases.
4. Decorate with a mimosa ball. Leave to set.

MUESLI & APRICOT CUPS

110 g (4 oz) plain cooking chocolate
15 ml (1 tbsp) syrup
80 g (3 oz) muesli

15 g ($^1/_2$ oz) chopped glacé cherries
15 g ($^1/_2$ oz) chopped dried apricots
small amount of angelica

1. Melt chocolate and syrup together, remove from heat and mix in cherries, apricots and muesli.
2. Put small amounts into sweet cases.
3. Decorate with small pieces of angelica.

CHOCOLATE 3-LAYER SANDWICH

225 g (8 oz) marzipan, or any confection firm enough to roll, eg. fondant
225 g (8 oz) rum truffle (see page 55)
slivers of crystallized fruit, flavoured as wished
110 g (4 oz) dark chocolate for coating

1. Roll out the marzipan into a rectangle 5 mm ($^1/_4$ inch) thick.
2. Press slivers of the fruit firmly into this base.
3. Spread chocolate paste over the fruit.
4. Leave to harden, about one hour.
5. Cut into evenly-sized pieces with a sharp knife – squares, triangles, diamonds, rectangles.
6. Separate and leave to harden.
7. Melt chocolate for coating. Dip the chocolates.
8. Leave to cool slightly before decorating with a pattern.

UNCOOKED SWEETS

Children enjoy sweet-making mainly for the end product (so do adults!), but apart from the immediate pleasure, there are more fundamental benefits as well. They learn about ingredients, flavours and measurements, and the process helps them to develop their creativity. Uncooked sweets are an ideal introduction to the subject.

MINT CREAMS

225 g (8 oz) icing sugar
egg albumen

3 drops peppermint oil
5 ml (1 tsp) glycerine

1. Sieve icing sugar, add essence to taste with glycerine.
2. Work in sufficient egg white to a rollable paste.
3. Cut into small circles, dry at room temperature.
4. Either dip half or whole in melted chocolate if wished.

NUT CHOCOLATE LAYERS
(makes 50–60)

225 g (8 oz) hazelnuts
5–10 ml (1–2 tsp) honey
225 g (8 oz) white chocolate
15 ml (1 tbsp) Grand Marnier

110 g (4 oz) caster sugar
450 g (1 lb) plain chocolate
22.5 ml (1½ tbsp) Kirsch

1. Mix nuts, sugar and honey in blender until a soft paste is achieved.
2. Chop half plain chocolate and melt. Melt white chocolate separately.
3. Beat half nut paste into each bowl of melted chocolate.
4. Add Kirsch to the plain chocolate, and Grand Marnier to the white chocolate.
5. Divide each in half and roll out between clingfilm (4 layers altogether).
6. Chill for 10 minutes.
7. Stack layers alternately. Trim edges.
8. Cut into 4 cm (1½ ins) strips.
9. Grate remaining chocolate and melt.
10. Spread over strips.
11. Leave on greaseproof paper to set. Cut with oiled knife.

CHOCOLATE RAISIN CUPS

55 g (2 oz) seedless raisins
30 ml (2 tbsp) rum or brandy

80 g (3 oz) plain chocolate
12–14 sweet cases

1. Soak raisins in rum or brandy for as long as possible, overnight at least.
2. Place sweet cases in twos. Using a brush, coat the inside of the cases with melted chocolate and allow to set.
3. Fill cases with raisin mixture. Run melted chocolate over to form filled cups.
4. Allow to set overnight and peel off paper cases.

   Note: Try other fillings; eg. fondant, marzipan, rum truffle, Turkish delight.

APRICOT CONFECTION

225 g (8 oz) dried apricots
110 g (4 oz) seedless raisins
110 g (4 oz) stoned prunes

5 ml (1 tsp) finely grated orange zest
15–30 ml (1–2 tbsp) runny honey / syrup
80 g (3 oz) granulated sugar
                or chopped nuts

1. Mince together thoroughly the dried fruit, or use a food processor to reduce the dried fruit to a paste.
2. Add grated zest and work in just enough honey or syrup to bind the mixture.
3. Form small spoonfuls of the mixture into balls, and roll the balls in granulated sugar or chopped nuts.
4. Allow sweets to dry in the atmosphere for 12–24 hours.

Note: Any mixture of dried fruits can be combined. Small amounts of ground spices like cinnamon or cloves give interesting variations.

COCONUT & CHERRY PETITS FOURS

55 g (2 oz) unsalted butter
55 g (2 oz) icing sugar
110 g (4 oz) coating chocolate

25 g (1 oz) chopped cherries
80 g (3 oz) dessicated coconut

1. Soften the butter, beat in the sugar and add coconut and cherries.
2. Form into balls (approx. 18), leave to harden in refrigerator.
3. Dip in melted chocolate and place on foil or silicone paper to dry.

ALMOND TRUFFLES

55 g (2 oz) ground almonds   15 ml (1 tbsp) sherry
55 g (2 oz) caster sugar   7.5 ml (1$\frac{1}{2}$ level tsp) apricot jam
55 g (2 oz) Nice biscuits made into fine crumbs

For coating:
chocolate flakes, grated chocolate and/or chocolate powder

1. Put the ground almonds, sugar and biscuit crumbs together in a bowl and mix well. Add the jam and sherry and bind all together.
2. Divide into small pieces, approx. 25–30 pieces, roll into barrel shapes and then roll in flakes and chocolate powder.
3. Should be eaten within 8 days of making.

ORANGE CHOCOLATE CUPS
(makes 12)

110 g (4 oz) plain chocolate   15 ml (1 tbsp) orange juice or Cointreau
55 g (2 oz) cake crumbs   orange food colouring (optional)
15 ml (1 level tbsp) ground almonds   25 g (1 oz) white chocolate
15 ml (1 level tbsp) icing sugar   12 petits fours cases
grated rind of half orange

1. Coat petits fours cases with chocolate and allow to set.
2. Mix cake crumbs, ground almonds, icing sugar and orange rind.
3. Add orange juice or Cointreau and mix to a stiff paste.
4. Fill the chocolate cases with the mixture, smooth the top and cover the top with the remaining melted chocolate.
5. Stir a little food colouring into the white chocolate and place in a piping bag. Fold down the top of the bag and snip off the end to allow the chocolate to come through in a thin line.
6. Pipe a spiral on top of each chocolate and drag a cocktail stick across to create a feathered effect.
7. Keep in an airtight container for up to one week.

Note: The above ingredients can be increased in quantity per ingredient, and used in Queen Cake cases as a dessert. Replace the white chocolate with cream.

ALMOND BONBONS

110 g (4 oz) stale sponge or Madeira cake   orange flower water
225 g (8 oz) sugar   extra icing sugar for coating
225 g (8 oz) ground almonds

1. Crush cake into fine crumbs, sift icing sugar and add to ground almonds.
2. Add sufficient orange flower water to make a stiff paste.
3. Shape into balls and roll in sifted icing sugar.

FRUIT PASTES

Uncooked fruit pastes are generally made from dried apricots, dates, prunes or combinations of these with other dried fruits, sultanas, raisins, etc., and nuts. The processed or minced fruits and nuts are bound with a syrup in some form, more usually with honey. All the ingredients are bound together until a satisfactory texture is achieved. If it seems too dry, it can be moistened with a little extra syrup or lemon juice. If it is too moist, add ground nuts or icing sugar.

If melted chocolate is used to bind the ingredients, the result will be similar to the FRUIT AND NUT TRUFFLES on page 54.

Fruit pastes are better classed as 'sweetmeats' rather than 'sweets'. This implies they are more usually eaten on the same day, at the end of a meal, and are not generally included in an assortment of sweets and candies intended for keeping.

APRICOT PASTE

150 g (5 oz) dried apricots   2.5 ml ($^1/_2$ tsp) grated lemon rind
40 g (1$^1/_2$ oz) dessicated coconut   lemon juice (if mixture seems dry)
15 g ($^1/_2$ oz) mixed nuts   sugar for coating
2.5 ml ($^1/_2$ tsp) grated orange rind

1. If the apricots are not the 'ready to eat' type and seem rather hard and dry, steam them for about 5 minutes, then put all the ingredients, except the lemon juice, through a mincer or food processor.
2. Add lemon juice if the paste seems dry.
3. When thoroughly mixed, shape into balls and roll in sugar – caster or granulated.

MICROWAVE SWEETS

Many traditional recipes can be cooked in the microwave.

GENERAL GUIDANCE
1. Use a pyrex bowl. Make sure it is large enough for the mixture to rise.
2. Use a sugar thermometer to check temperature.
3. Use oven gloves to handle the bowl.
4. Always place bowl on a dry cloth or surface on removing from microwave.

COFFEE GANACHE

1 egg yolk	coffee essence
25 g (1 oz) caster sugar	200 g (7 oz) plain chocolate for dipping
100 ml (4 fl oz) single cream	7 g ($^1/_4$ oz) vegetable fat
225 g (8 oz) plain chocolate	

1. Mix egg yolk, sugar and cream together in a bowl.
2. Cook on MEDIUM for 3 minutes or until the custard has thickened, stirring at one-minute intervals.
3. Melt the chocolate, blend into the custard with the coffee essence.
4. Using a balloon whisk, whisk until smooth. Leave to cool.
5. Melt 200 g (7 oz) plain chocolate and vegetable fat, and form ganache balls.
6. Coat by dipping into chocolate *or* pipe into coated petits fours cases and cover with melted chocolate.

CASHEW OR BRAZIL NUT CRUNCH

225 g (8 oz) granulated sugar	knob of butter, hazelnut size
200 g (7 oz) golden syrup	5 ml (1 tsp) vanilla essence
150 g (5 oz) cashew/Brazil nuts, chopped	5 ml (1 tsp) baking powder

1. Blend the sugar and syrup. Cook on HIGH for 4 minutes.
2. Add the nuts. Stir and cook on HIGH for 2–3 minutes.
3. Add the butter and essence. Stir well. Cook on HIGH for 1 minute.
4. Sprinkle the baking powder over the mixture, stir gently until foamy.
5. Spread the mixture on to silicone paper. Cool and cut into pieces.
6. Store in an airtight container.

COCONUT ICE

225 g (8 oz) desiccated coconut
55 g (2 oz) butter
225 ml (8 fl oz) evaporated milk

55 g (2 oz) granulated sugar
few drops of colouring (pink)

1. Spread coconut on a plate. Cook full power for 4 minutes, stirring frequently.
2. Put butter, milk and sugar into a large bowl. Cook at full power for 3 minutes.
3. Stir and cook again for 4 minutes.
4. Stir in the coconut and food colouring, press into a 15 x 20 cm (6 x 8 ins) microwave dish, cook at full power for 3 minutes.
5. Press mixture down again and set aside to cool before cutting into bars.

CHOCOLATE FUDGE

110 g (4 oz) plain chocolate
55 g (2 oz) butter
45 ml (3 tbsp) evaporated milk

few drops vanilla essence
450 g (1 lb) sifted icing sugar

1. Break up the chocolate and put in a bowl with butter and milk.
2. Cook on HIGH for 90 seconds.
3. Stir and cook for a further 90 seconds.
4. Blend in the vanilla essence and the sifted icing sugar.
5. Press into a buttered tin 15 x 20 cm (6 x 8 ins) and leave to set.
6. Cut into squares or blocks.

COFFEE FUDGE

450 g (1 lb) sifted icing sugar
218 g (7½ oz) can condensed milk
30 ml (2 tbsp) golden syrup

55 g (2 oz) butter
15 ml (1 tbsp) water
15 ml (1 tbsp) Camp coffee

1. Mix all the ingredients into a large bowl, cook uncovered on DEFROST for 10 minutes, stirring four times.
2. Cook on full power for 7 minutes or until it reaches 116°C/240°F. Remove from oven.
3. Beat until mixture begins to thicken and grain.
4. Pour into an oiled 18 cm (7 ins) square tin.
5. Mark into squares when cool, cut when cold.

TRUFFLES

80 g (3 oz) chocolate
15 g (½ oz) butter
1 egg yolk, beaten
10 ml (2 tsp) cream

15–30 ml (1–2 tbsp) rum
80 g (3 oz) icing sugar
25 g (1 oz) chopped nuts
    or chocolate vermicelli

1. Put chocolate and butter in a bowl. Cook on HIGH for one minute in microwave.
2. Add the beaten egg. Blend thoroughly and cook on MEDIUM for 2 minutes.
3. Blend in the cream, rum and sugar.
4. Allow to cool slightly, form into balls and coat. To coat, put the nuts or vermicelli in a small polythene or paper bag, toss the truffles individually. Tossing more than one truffle at a time will result in loss of shape. Do not put used nuts or vermicelli back in storage jars with unused ingredients.

GINGER TRUFFLES

25 g (1 oz) butter
30 ml (1 fl oz) double cream
80 g (3 oz) plain chocolate, grated
½ egg yolk

25 g (1 oz) stem ginger, chopped
15 ml (1 tbsp) Drambuie
cocoa powder

1. Cook butter and cream on HIGH for 1½ minutes.
2. Stir in the grated chocolate and egg yolk. Cook on MEDIUM for 2 minutes.
3. Blend in the ginger and Drambuie. Cool.
4. Shape and coat in cocoa powder.

CHOCOLATE CHERRY TRUFFLES

150 g (5 oz) dark chocolate
55 g (2 oz) butter
350 g (12 oz) plain cake crumbs
110 g (4 oz) glacé or maraschino
    cherries, chopped

110 g (4 oz) icing sugar
30–45 ml (2–3 tbsp) rum or orange juice
chocolate vermicelli, chocolate drinking
    powder, icing sugar, grated
    chocolate to finish

1. Place chocolate and butter in a large bowl. Cook on HIGH for 2 minutes.
2. Stir in remaining ingredients. Place in fridge to cool until firm to handle.
3. Form into balls and roll in vermicelli or chocolate powder, etc.
4. Put in sweet cases.

NUT CARAMELS

150 g (5 oz) clear honey
80 g (3 oz) butter
55 g (2 oz) chopped mixed nuts, or one kind only
150 g (5 oz) golden syrup

1. Place butter in a large bowl and cook uncovered for one minute on HIGH.
2. Stir in syrup and honey and cook for 9 minutes on HIGH or until 132°C/270°F. Stir once.
3. Beat until thick and add chopped nuts.
4. Pour into oiled tin 18 cm (7 ins) square.
5. When caramel has nearly set and is cool enough to handle, take a teaspoon of the mixture and form into balls. Flatten slightly, place on oiled foil and leave to set hard overnight. Wrap in cellophane.

CHOCOLATE NUT MARZIPAN

110 g (4 oz) marzipan
80 g (3 oz) plain chocolate
25 g (1 oz) finely chopped nuts
drinking chocolate or finely grated chocolate

1. Break up chocolate and marzipan into small pieces. Place in microwave and cook on HIGH for 3 minutes.
2. Remove from microwave and mix thoroughly.
3. Return for one minute on full.
4. Cool. Add chopped nuts and knead together. Roll into balls and dust with drinking chocolate.

CHOCOLATE PEPPERMINT CRISPS

110 g (4 oz) plain chocolate   25 g (1 oz) Demerara sugar
4 drops oil of peppermint

1. Melt the chocolate on MEDIUM for 1 minute. Add the oil of peppermint.
2. Spread on silicone paper 3 mm ($^1/_8$ inch) thick.
3. Sprinkle with the Demerara sugar.
4. Allow to cool and cut into matchsticks or squares or triangles.

PRALINE

55 g (2 oz) whole almonds
110 g (4 oz) granulated sugar

1. Mix the almonds and sugar on a double sheet of greaseproof paper that fits the turntable. Microwave on HIGH for 5–8 minutes, stirring every minute until all the sugar is melted and a brown syrup forms. Leave to cool.
2. Break up the almond brittle and store in an airtight jar. Small pieces can be processed in food processor and used in ice-cream, etc.

BARRELOS

Almond Paste
110 g (4 oz) icing sugar
110 g (4 oz) ground almonds

25 g (1 oz) reconstituted egg albumen
5 ml (1 tsp) orange flower water

Chocolate
45 ml (3 tbsp) double cream
15 g (½ oz) butter
15 ml (1 tbsp) water

110 g (4 oz) plain chocolate
cornflour

Coating: **25 g (1 oz) granulated sugar**

1. Blend together ingredients for almond paste.
2. Divide into four pieces for ease of handling. Form into sausage shapes. With a rolling pin, roll to oblong shape 5 cm (2 ins) wide. Trim the edges.
3. Put the cream in a bowl. Microwave on HIGH for ½–1 minute.
4. Stir in the butter and 15 ml (1 tbsp) water. Microwave on HIGH for one minute.
5. Add the broken chocolate pieces. Microwave on HIGH for 2 minutes.
6. Blend the mixture thoroughly. Cool until the mixture begins to thicken.
7. Work into a malleable paste.
8. Divide the chocolate mixture into 4 equal pieces and roll in cornflour to form ropes the length of the almond paste.
9. Place in the centre of the almond paste and roll up the long sides to enclose the chocolate. Cut into 1 cm (½ inch) square pieces.
10. Roll in granulated sugar. Store in an airtight tin.

VARIATION:
For a mocha filling, blend 15 g (½ oz) coffee powder with the water.

PACKAGING AND PRESENTATION

The final stage in sweet-making is, of course, attractive presentation. Many sweets and toffees may be packed in screw-topped or stoppered glass jars and look especially attractive if the colours are glowing and the texture crystalline. Other sweets, such as caramels, must be protected from exposure to air, as this could make them sticky.

Wax paper and cellophane

Wax paper and cellophane, cut into suitably sized squares, are ideal for this and both can be obtained from good stationers. If you have access to a WI Country Market you may be able to purchase rolls of cellophane from them, if you have difficulty finding them elsewhere; and they do make use of sheets of 'Butcher's Wrap', which is also satisfactory.

It may be worthwhile approaching a local wholesale paper and packaging supplier who will be prepared to sell to you on a personal basis. I have tried this and have been able to purchase rolls of cellophane and cellophane bags which are perfect for fudge (though these have to be bought by the 1000), for card for making boxes, and an endless selection of fancy ribbons for decoration.

Glacine Paper

Chocolates should be presented in boxes, sitting in individual fluted paper cases to protect them from bruising. The chocolate-coloured waxy cases are made from 'glacine paper'. I have purchased sheets of glacine paper from 'Paperchase' in Tottenham Court Road, London. This is used to line boxes and to separate layers of chocolates if necessary. The glacine paper cases are obtainable from

Sugarcraft shops. They are usually sold in small quantities of 25 or so but if you intend to produce larger quantities these cases come from the manufacturer in packs of 1000 and can work out much cheaper if you can persuade your Sugarcraft supplier to let you have them.

Boxes for sweets

Purchasing suitable boxes to package your sweets can be difficult. Apart from being expensive, it is difficult to find a size which is exactly right for the purpose and it can be frustrating to find that the box you have chosen will not accommodate all you intend to put in it or, worse still, has space left over and there are no more sweets or chocolates left to fill it!

Padding for boxes

For a box which is slightly deeper than its contents, it will be necessary to insert some kind of padding to prevent the contents from shifting. New plastic 'bubble wrap' used to wrap fragile items and even to insulate greenhouses is perfect. It is obtainable from DIY stores. Also available from stationers is finely shredded tissue paper. This, as well as the 'bubble wrap' can be placed over or under the contents of your box.

Home-made boxes

In view of the cost of buying ready-made boxes, it can be very worthwhile and rewarding to construct your own. The following ideas are based mainly on shapes and therefore involve very few actual measurements. These are given where necessary. All the boxes can be made either from an A4-sized sheet of card (obtainable from stationers) or from the 'food card' supplied in WI Markets. This is a very high-grade card with a grease-resistant coating on one or both sides; it measures 203 x 160 mm (8 x 6 3/8 ins).

SIMPLE BOX WITH A LID

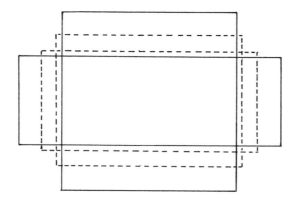

You will need firm card and suitable covering paper.

1. Decide the dimensions of the box, square or rectangular. Draw the base shape carefully and add the depth of the four sides all round. Repeat this for the lid, remembering that the centre shape will be 2–3 mm ($^1/_{16}$–$^1/_8$ inch) larger all round, and the depth will be shallower. In the diagram, the solid lines are the box shape, the dotted lines are the lid.
2. Cut out in card and score round the centre shape.
3. Glue both shapes to the covering paper and cut out, allowing 10–15 mm ($^1/_2$–$^5/_8$ inch) extra all round. Snip into the corners, fold and glue the flaps of paper over the short ends of the card.
4. Fold up the sides of the card and glue the remaining flaps of paper to the adjacent sides.
5. Fold in and glue down the remaining top edges.
6. The box and lid may be lined with appropriate paper, using the basic shape as a guide. Decorate with a fancy bow or ribbon.

THE PILLOW PACK

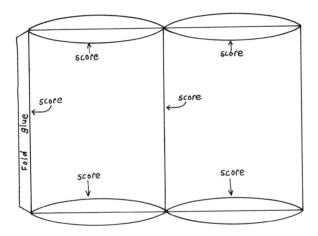

This can be made to any size.

1. Using the diagram as a guide, carefully draw two rectangles of the size required, side by side. Add approx 1 cm ($^1/_2$ inch) for a flap. Using a postcard as the size, this will make a container 14 x 10 cm ($5^1/_2$ x 4 ins) which will hold about 110 g (4 oz) sweets.
2. Using a teaplate or saucer as a guide, cut the outer curves and score the inner curves. Score the two vertical lines. Cut out the complete shape.
3. Bend on the straight scored lines and glue down the flap.
4. Wait until this is completely dry, then gently press in the curved scored ends.

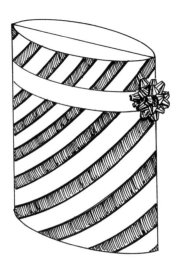

THE CONE PACK

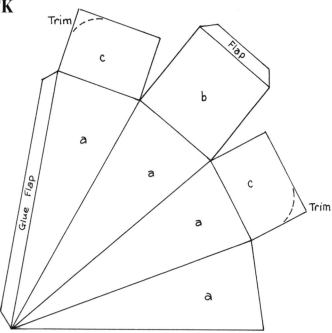

This is based on four equal triangles laid side by side, two extended with side flaps and one with a closing flap.

1. Using the diagram as a guide, draw a narrow triangle. The apex must be opposite the centre of the base. A useful size is 20 cm (8 ins) high and 6 cm (2½ ins) at the base.
2. Draw three more triangle shapes adjacent to the first (shapes 'a' in the diagram), one with a flap along the outer side.
3. Draw a square on one of the sections and add a flap (shape 'b').
4. Add rectangles on each side of shape 'b' and trim to a curved shape as shown (shapes 'c').
5. Score all straight lines and bend the cone into shape.
6. Glue the flap to seal.

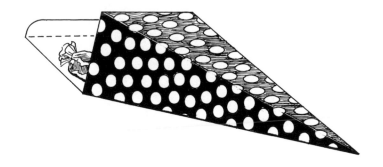

THE BON BON BOX

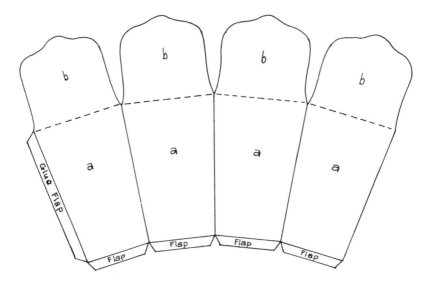

This is based on four rectangles slightly narrowed at one end.

1. Decide on the height and width of the box and cut a rectangle to these measurements in card. 10 x 6 cm (4 x 2½ ins) is a useful size. Narrow the rectangle slightly at one end, taking an equal amount from each side. This will give you shape 'a'.
2. Copy 4 of these shapes side by side on your box card. Add flaps where shown.
3. Sketch a curved shape that will form the top flaps 'b' and draw on to the wide ends of the shapes 'a'.
4. Cut out the completed shape.
5. Score the vertical lines and the base lines. Do NOT score the dotted lines.
6. Bend into shape and glue the long flap in place.
7. Bend in the base flaps, cut a square of card the size of the base, glue in place.
8. When the contents are in the pack, gently bend over the top flaps – do not crease.
9. Seal with a ribbon or bow.

INGREDIENTS INDEX

INGREDIENTS INDEX

INGREDIENTS INDEX

INGREDIENTS INDEX

INGREDIENTS INDEX

INGREDIENTS INDEX

ABOUT THE WI

If you have enjoyed this book, the chances are that you would enjoy belonging to the largest women's organisation in the country – the National Federation of Women's Institutes, or the WI as it is usually known.

We are friendly, go-ahead, like-minded women, who derive enormous satisfaction from all the movement has to offer. The list is long – you can make new friends, have fun and companionship, visit new places, develop new skills, take part in community services, fight local campaigns, become a WI Market producer, and play an active rôle in an organisation which has a national voice.

The WI is the only women's organisation in the country that owns an adult education establishment. At Denman College, you can take a course in anything from car maintenance to paper sculpture, from book binding to yoga, or cordon bleu cookery to fly fishing.

For more information, write to the **National Federation of Women's Institutes, 104 New Kings Road, London SW6 4LY, phone 0171-371-9300. The NFWI Wales Office is at 19 Cathedral Road, Cardiff CF1 9LJ, phone 01222-221712.**

MORE FROM WI BOOKS

There are lots more books on cookery and crafts available from WI Books, the WI's own publishing company. You can get hold of a catalogue from **WI Books, Glebe House, Church Street, Crediton, Devon EX17 2AF (01363-777575)**, or order titles direct from **WI Books, Biblios Distributors, Star Road, Partridge Green, West Sussex RH13 8LD (Tel. 01403-710971)**.

Note especially other titles in the new **"WI Books of ..."** cookery series:

Bread and Bakes by Kay Bradley
Cooking for One by Margaret Foss
Jams and Preserves by Pat Hesketh
Salsas and Unusual Preserves by Grace Mulligan
A Taste of WI Markets edited by Midge Thomas

Still available from the original series: **Biscuits, Cakes, Fish and Seafood, Microwave Cookery, Pastry, Soups and Starters, Vegetables and Salads**.

ABOUT THE COMPILERS

MARGARET CLIFT is a member of Frindsbury WI and Frindsbury Extra WI in the West Kent Federation. Margaret attended Hadlow College, Kent, and obtained Home Economics certificates in bakery, wine-making and preservation; she went on to qualify as a National Federation Home Economics judge, tutor and demonstrator. She has also obtained National Federation craft certificates in patchwork, dressmaking, gloving and flower arranging, culminating in tutor and judges certificates.

She currently provides tutorials, demonstrations and lectures to Women's Institutes, schools, clubs and horticultural societies in the county, as well as at the annual county show.

IRENE GREEN trained to teach modern and classical languages. She has always had a keen interest in all forms of craftwork and cooking, and obtained the City & Guilds certificate in needlwork and dressmaking. She settled in West Sussex in 1965 and joined the WI and WI Market in Selsey. Through the WI she attended an adult education course in sweet and chocolate making.

She has served as President of Selsey Manor WI, Chairman of Selsey WI Market, and Chairman of West Sussex WI Markets. She has also served as Chairman of Home Economics and as Publications Officer on the Executive of West Sussex Federation.

For about 20 years, she has enjoyed teaching and demonstrating the making of hand-made chocolates and decorative gift boxes to WIs and other similar groups across the south of England.

DILWEN PHILLIPS is a member of St Athan WI in Glamorgan. Currently she is an NFWI Officer and Chairman of WI Books. She trained as a Home Economist in Cardiff, and taught in schools and Further Education colleges in Wales. She is a former tutor at Denman College and a former cookery judge, judge tutor and assessor.

Dilwen says that her family loved making sweets when they were children and her grandchildren enjoy making them now; there are always home-made sweets at a family gathering.